Crafting Multimedia Text

Websites and Presentations

BARBARA MORAN
Cañada College
San Francisco State University

NETEFFECT SERIES

PEARSON

Prentice
Hall

Upper Saddle River, New Jersey

Library of Congress Cataloging-in-Publication Data

Moran, Barbara
  Crafting multimedia text: websites and presentations / Barbara Moran.
    p. cm.—(NetEffect series)
  ISBN 0-13-099002-7
  1. Interactive multimedia—Authorship. 2. World Wide Web. 3. Web sites—Design. I. Title. II. Series.

QA76.76.I59M667 2004
006.7′8—dc22   2004009537

Director of Production and Manufacturing: Bruce Johnson
Executive Editor: Elizabeth Sugg
Editorial Assistant: Cyrenne Bolt de Freitas
Marketing Manager: Leigh Ann Sims
Marketing Editor-Production: Mary Carnis
Manufacturing Buyer: Ilene Sanford
Production Liaison: Denise Brown
Full-Service Production: Gay Pauley/Holcomb Hathaway
Composition: Carlisle Communications, Ltd.
Design Director: Cheryl Asherman
Senior Design Coordinator/Cover Design: Christopher Weigand
Cartoons: David Watson
Cover Printer: Phoenix Color
Printer/Binder: Phoenix Book Tech Park

Pearson Education Ltd.   Pearson Education Australia Pty. Limited
Pearson Education Singapore Pte. Ltd.   Pearson Education North Asia Ltd.
Pearson Education Canada, Ltd.   Pearson Educación de Mexico, S. A. de C.V.
Pearson Education—Japan   Pearson Education Malaysia Pte. Ltd.

10 9 8 7 6 5 4 3 2 1
ISBN 0-13-099002-7

Contents

Preface

This book is the result of the Business Communications course I teach at Cañada College in San Mateo County, California. Business Dean Linda Hayes and Professors Romelia Thiele and Carolyn Jung realized that business professionals need to write effective content for websites, slide presentations, and even e-mails. So in addition to teaching traditional methods of paper-based business writing, I was encouraged to build the multimedia writing component for business students.

The challenge was finding a supplemental book geared to multimedia writing. I couldn't. So I wrote this one.

Much of what I learned about multimedia writing was through working for two search engines and various Websites in the mid-1990s. I was especially fortunate to work for Christine Maxwell, now an Internet content consultant and Senior Partner at ISS, the Institute for Scientific Simulation in Monterey, California. She was a pioneer in adapting the best of print writing to the realities of multimedia.

Early on, it became obvious that writing for the computer screen was much different than writing for paper. There were no style guides for multimedia writers, so I began one.

I followed the early research of Jakob Nielsen, Ph.D., User Advocate and principal of the Nielsen Norman Group (co-founded with Dr. Donald A. Norman, a former VP of Research at Apple Computer). Until 1998 Nielsen was a Sun Microsystems Distinguished Engineer and a man called "the guru of Web page usability" by *The New York Times* in 1998. His work is cited in this book.

The final elements came together through my association with the Department of Instructional Technology in the School of Education at San Francisco State University. Then Chair Eugene Michaels, Ph.D.; current Chair Kim Foreman, Ph.D.; Professor Peggy Benton, Ph.D.; and lecturer Mary Scott helped me integrate learning theory, technology, and design with all my notes about writing I had been taking since 1996. What I learned from them is integral to this book. Usability expert Lynn R. Raiser, whom I met at the Department of Instructional Technology, provided valuable assistance with the CD-ROM for this book.

ACKNOWLEDGMENTS

I would like to thank the following reviewers for their constructive comments: Angelica Cortes, University of Texas Pan American; Diane Chute, Portland Community College; and Barry Maid, Arizona State University.

Special thanks to my editor, Elizabeth Sugg, who gave me the perfect blend of creative freedom and literary guidance. Her enthusiasm and professionalism mirrored that of the entire Prentice Hall team.

Prior to leaving traditional journalism, I worked with writers and editors whose talents and ideals (and humor) motivated and inspired me: colleagues at the *Atlanta Journal-Constitution*, the *San Diego Union*, and WGST News Radio in Atlanta; J. D. Alexander (who later became publisher of the *Seattle Post-Intelligencer*); Jon Funabiki (now deputy director of the Media, Arts and Culture unit at the Ford Foundation); Steve Droessler (a veteran editor at the *San Diego Union*); John Muncie (aka John Jaffe, who along with wife Jody Jaffe recently wrote *Thief of Words*); Steve Padilla (now deputy Metro Editor at *The Los Angeles Times*); Robert Rohrer (a veteran news editor at the *Atlanta Journal-Constitution*); Jim Bentley (former managing editor, now retired, of Cox News Service); Carl Cannon (now with the *National Journal*); Eric Seidel (now of The Media Trainers); Fred Muir (later of *The Los Angeles Times*); Mike Wheeler (now with Westerly Partners); Bill Stothers (now Deputy Director of The Center for an Accessible Society); Forrest Sawyer (now anchoring for NBC and MSNBC); and those departed—Fay S. Joyce, Jerry Schwartz, Barbara Williams, and humorist Lewis Grizzard.

Two teachers inspired me to devote my life to writing. One was Harvey Saalberg, my journalism professor at Kent State University in the mid-70s. The other was Joanne Zimmer Bonno, my fifth-grade teacher, who first encouraged me to write back in the early 60s when she was just starting her teaching career. She retired in 2001 as Director of Student Teaching Programs at the College of Mount St. Joseph.

This book is dedicated to the ones I love communicating with most: my husband G. Robert Baker, Ph.D.; son Christopher "CJ" Baker; all my nieces and nephews; Steve Dibble; Irene McCormack; Vanessa and Lydia Jackson; Deborah and John Morrow, Ph.D.; Bill R. Adams; and my grandkids Allyson and Rachael Cook. Finally, I remember my late father, Arthur George Moran, who taught me to value and respect words, especially those delivered with kindness.

About the Author

Barbara Moran spent 20 years in "mainstream news" (as editor of a city magazine and a weekly newspaper, on-air radio news reporter, and staff writer for *San Diego Union* and *Atlanta Constitution*). In 1989, she left traditional media to become part of the new Web-based media. She worked for two search engines as an online editor, and she has freelanced extensively online. She wrote *The Internet Directory for Kids & Parents* (IDG Books) and contributed a chapter on multimedia writing to *English for Careers: Business, Professional, and Technical* by Leila Smith (Prentice Hall). Founder/editor of her own K–12 educational Website (www.specialspecies.com), Ms. Moran serves as a communications consultant and teaches Internet-, computer-, and communications-related subjects at the college level (at San Francisco State University and San Mateo Community College District). She has her B.A. in telecommunications from Kent State University and her master's in instructional technology from the School of Education at San Francisco State University. To contact her consulting service, email msbmoran@yahoo.com.

Introduction

Within the last 10 years, the practice of presenting written information on a screen rather than on paper has grown dramatically. The essence of multimedia communications lies in its interactivity and the way that writing occurs in layers rather than in a linear, traditional style.

For those who may be "Trekkies," I compare multimedia writing to the three-dimensional chess game that Mr. Spock liked to play on *Star Trek*. Unlike traditional chess, which is played on a flat, two-dimensional surface, his tri-d chess is a three-dimensional game that requires players to consider moves on a multidimensional platform. Not only must they consider the linear move in front of them, but they must also anticipate the impact of those moves on separate, clear boards located above and below the main board. Each piece impacts a number of levels. Players have to remain aware of how every piece on every level interrelates.

This reminds me of the challenge of multimedia writing. Not only must we ponder the linear story we are writing on the main level, but we must also consider upper and lower levels accessible by hyperlinks or mouse clicks. We have to think about how each word connects to words on screens not yet visible. It is a form of three-dimensional writing that we are only beginning to comprehend, much less master. Just as in the chess game, in multimedia communication each piece of information impacts a number of levels, and writers have to remain aware of how every level interrelates.

The computer screen—through the development of Websites and presentation software such as Microsoft PowerPoint—is now used interchangeably with paper as a medium for information.

With that in mind, here are some of the issues we will explore in this book:

- What types of information are more suited for output to the computer screen vs. paper?
- How does reading information on paper compare with viewing written information on a computer screen (or projector screen)?
- Should information be presented in the same way for paper as for the computer screen?
- Are currently accepted multimedia emphasis techniques (such as moving text) enhancements or distractions?

Research into these areas is new, but certain conventions have emerged. This book will examine the current state-of-the-art implementation of multimedia writing. It will show differences between viewers (those who see information projected on a screen) and readers (those who read information on paper).

Giving conscious thought to these differences goes a long way toward helping instructional designers, Website developers, educators, journalists, and businesspeople build effective communication with clients, students, and the public at large.

This book is geared to students and professionals in business, design, education, and mass communications. It is a cross-curricular book that can stand alone as a teaching tool or be integrated into any curriculum. It is not a book on technical writing, nor does it focus on creating text for output to paper. It is a unique book addressing a new and unique form of writing. Whether or not you are a professional writer, this book will help you.

Outputting text to a computer screen rather than to paper is a content revolution that began in earnest when desktop computers were developed. Now, just about anyone can publish text. The challenge is can they publish good text?

I began my career as a writer/editor in 1973 in traditional communications: news radio and weekly and daily newspapers. In 1996, I switched to multimedia, working for an Internet start-up. I was no longer known as a writer/editor even though I was doing those jobs. The multimedia world had new titles for everyone (or so it seemed). I became a "content provider." In positions since, I have been termed an instructional designer, a learning strategist, a project manager, a content designer, and an editorial director.

The truth is, I'm still writing and editing. But the medium is different. I no longer write articles; now I create content. I'm not writing words; now I'm inputting text or copy. Essentially, it's still writing, only in a different form.

Starting in 1998, I began teaching both traditional and multimedia communications at the college level. Through my experience in both traditional and "new" media, I have gathered insights about what works and what doesn't. I have learned from respected designers, educators, and communications specialists.

Too often in the past, written content was treated as an afterthought, rather than the central reason for a Website or multimedia presentation. A lot of grand-looking computer-based presentations left visitors/viewers befuddled because the words failed to guide them.

We know now that when multimedia content is presented effectively, good things happen:

- Students acquire new and lasting knowledge.
- Customers build loyal relationships with business professionals.
- Clients are happy with Web designs.
- The public gets useful, timely information and returns for more.
- Employees grasp new policies and instruction readily.

This is not a book to teach writing. Rather it is meant to teach effective ways to present narrative and informational text on a computer screen—be it the text for a Website, CD-ROM, or on-screen presentation such as PowerPoint.

This book examines word choice, style, tone, editing, and visual presentation of multimedia text. While writing for multimedia is different than writing print documents or film/video scripts, it incorporates elements of both.

In the course of reading this book, you will:

- Examine, evaluate, and understand the differences between writing traditional documents (print-based) and writing for multimedia (electronic-based).
- Place emphasis on proper business English, and on creating and formatting multimedia content with impact. Whether they're for business, news, or education, well-crafted slide shows and Websites deserve intelligent, lively, accurate, and appealing text.
- Learn why traditional writing skills don't always translate well to the computer screen.
- See what techniques will help you write like a top professional for this ever-expanding communications medium.
- Understand how to legally protect your content; look at the ethics and legalities of writing for, and taking content from, Websites.
- Find out how to properly cite sources, avoid plagiarism, and assess the credibility of content on the Web.
- Determine the best ways to present your written content on a screen.
- Explore the written components of Websites and multimedia presentations; get a brief history of multimedia communications and find out what the future holds.

You do not need to know PowerPoint, HTML, or Web-authoring software to benefit from this book. This is a nontechnical approach to modern writing in a high-tech environment. You do need to have good basic writing skills, and know how to key and use word-processing software.

This book is designed for both writers and nonwriters in the fields of business, design, journalism, and education. It will prove useful to anyone trying to establish a high-quality on-screen style that provides a consistent approach and image, as well as a professional touch. It will increase your chances for success in the ever-evolving arena of multimedia communications.

Let this book unleash your creativity and confidence as a multimedia writer. :-)

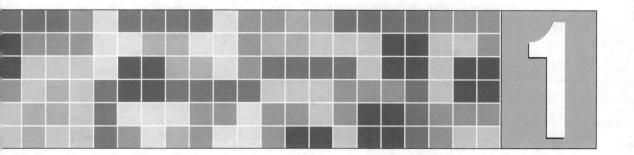

What Is Multimedia Writing?

It is with words as with sunbeams, the more they are condensed, the deeper they burn.

— Robert Southey, English poet (1774–1843)

OBJECTIVES

This chapter will help you learn:

- What constitutes multimedia
- What constitutes multimedia writing
- How multimedia developed
- Where multimedia writing stands today
- The future of multimedia writing

The Real Birth of Multimedia Writing

WHAT CONSTITUTES MULTIMEDIA?

Just 10 years ago, *multimedia* was a cutting-edge term. Even now, it has various meanings. In the world of computing, it tends to mean any presentation combining copy, images, sound, and motion. It usually also utilizes hypertext (clickable links from one section to another, generally delineated with an underline and color different from the rest of the text).

Most significantly, multimedia presentations are outputted to a screen rather than to paper. An e-mail is an example of a basic multimedia presentation because it is written for and read on a screen rather than the paper medium of traditional correspondence. The personal computer has made the development and implementation of multimedia content a booming reality.

Simply put, *multi* means more than one, or many. *Multi* derives from the Latin *multus*, meaning *much*. *Media* is plural for *medium* and can be defined as a method of expression.

In art, for example, watercolors are a medium of expression. So are oil paints, acrylics, and pastels. In journalism, newspapers are a form of expression in the mass media. So is broadcasting. We have all heard the term *news media*, which means media for reporting news. There is TV news, radio news, print news, and now Internet news.

For the purposes of this book, we will define multimedia as any presentation that combines text display with sound, visuals, and motion. Primary examples include Websites, CD-ROMs, and on-screen slide presentations.

Multimedia communications generally involve three basic elements:

1. Information (content or text)
2. Visuals
3. Interactivity

This book focuses on multimedia presentations for business, education, the arts, and journalism. More than ever, people in these fields need to be able to communicate effectively in a multimedia world. For new Web developers, teachers, business, and communications professionals, understanding how to craft text for the computer screen is now a requirement.

WHAT CONSTITUTES MULTIMEDIA WRITING?

Society has established through the ages that people can learn through words. Language has existed since the dawn of humankind as the primary vehicle for education, communication, and enlightenment.

Modern society has also established that people can learn through technology. (Otherwise, the advertising industry would not spend millions every year on TV and Web ads.) Shows like *Sesame Street* and *Blue's Clues* are considered fine examples of technological teachers.

This book serves as an introduction to the power of combining technology with words—words with technology.

There are many books on writing. There are many books that teach the technical elements of putting up a Website, operating camera/editing equipment, or using slide presentation software (such as MS PowerPoint, iMovie, Apple Keynote, or Authorware). There are also many books on graphic design.

But there is not a lot of information available on how to write for the computer screen and how to present words (otherwise known as copy, text, or content) correctly in such an environment. Why is this?

It's not unusual for technological developments to precede the development of communications skills using that technology. The telephone was invented before we figured out how to carry on a conversation without actually looking at one another. Traditionally, eye contact was a big part of communication, but the telephone changed that and we had to figure out how to adapt our language skills. The telegraph and Morse code also preceded our ability to utilize them in some standardized fashion.

The mechanisms of communications technology tend to precede human conventions of use. The best communications technology needs a social dimension before it becomes really useful. Even a pencil is useless until a person writes with it.

Consider the development of TV. When television first began, it borrowed heavily from radio production style. In many ways, television was radio with pictures. At first, the novelty of seeing people on a screen while hearing them talk made television interesting. But over time, the novelty of this new technology began to fade. People had to begin developing content that was meaningful and unique to the television medium.

As a little girl in the 1950s, I used to watch my uncle who had one of the first television talk shows in America. Early on, the show—called "Breakfast Party"—consisted of people sitting on stools in front of microphones and talking to one another, much as they would on a radio broadcast. Visually, it was dull. And the radio-style writing seemed artificial and forced. It just didn't translate well to television.

Eventually, producers figured out how to develop attractive sets, costumes, and makeup (not needed in radio) as well as writing that fit the television medium. They let visuals rather than spoken adjectives tell the story. In radio, producers set a mood with music and sound effects. In television, they employed music and sound effects, but also lighting, staging, and camera angles. TV was growing well beyond its early radio-show model. Producers began taking their cameras outside the sound stage to actual remote locations. They experimented with audio, natural light, and filters in ways unknown to radio or even to movies.

One of the young writers on my uncle's staff was a guy named Rod Serling. He became a pioneer in terms of moving television from "radio with pictures" into its own dynamic communications medium. He created words, ideas, and content that fit the medium of television perfectly. As writer and executive producer of "The Twilight Zone," he showed what television could really be if people wrote specifically for it, rather than totally relying on earlier radio-show models.

So how does all this correlate with the modern development of multimedia? The original Internet, called ARPANET, originated in conjunction with the U.S. military and university research departments in the late 1960s. These entities primarily used it to transmit reports, research, statistical information, and other such documentation. ARPANET wasn't seen as its own new communications medium, but rather as a faster way to transmit information from traditional print documents.

Researcher Ray Tomlinson invented e-mail in the early 1970s for the same purpose—to transmit written messages and data quickly and easily.

Then in the 1980s and early 1990s came graphical user interfaces, hypertext markup language, browser development, and design software. When Tim Berners-Lee first launched the World Wide Web in 1991, it borrowed heavily from newspapers, reports, research papers, and magazine-style writing and presentation. In many ways, it was—and remains—newsprint with hyperlinks. It was more consumer-oriented but still locked in print-based traditions.

We are just now beginning the process of really exploring the potential of the Internet and World Wide Web (and whatever may come next) as a new, uncharted form of communication for business, education, and the arts.

Communication encompasses the "process of creating a meaning between two or more people."[1] Communications technology must further this, or it is just electronic machinery whose novelty and usefulness will fade.

Unfortunately, in many cases, "it is easier and more efficient to maintain current practices than to promulgate approaches for which significant shifts—epistemological, technological, cultural—are required. In truth, few designers have acknowledged, much less successfully negotiated, the hurdles associated with transforming a highly traditional community of educational practice."[2]

This book is an attempt to think about the way we use words and to recognize that words created for a computer screen must be presented much differently than words on paper if they are to be effective.

Serious attention must be paid to content basics, not just to layout, animation, images, graphics, and the other technological toys of the new computer universe. This is already happening. Consider the demise of many dot-coms. For a while, we were dazzled by all the new technology, but eventually we began to question the presentation of content and the usefulness of all these Web pages. Sixty million Web pages existed in the late 1990s, all following pretty much the standard print-style model. More colors, more flash, more razzamatazz, but still pretty much traditional print-style writing with hyperlinks.

Now people in multimedia have begun to realize the need to develop content that is truly meaningful and unique to multimedia. They understand that writing style and content credibility are just as important as a dancing logo.

A Website doesn't have to be just a book, a newspaper, or a mail-order catalog displayed on a screen. A slide show presentation doesn't have to be just a business or school report stuck like a photocopy onto a screen. Neither should they be blaring, glaring hodgepodge collections of fancy graphics combined with flat, obligatory words. Too often, words suffer at the expense of graphics.

When I teach Microsoft PowerPoint, I always require my students to write their entire scripts first—no effects, no graphics, just black text on a white background. They can size the text and arrange it on the slide, but that's it. It pained me when one student handed in her script and said, "I'm sorry it's so dry, but it just has words."

Viewing words as the automatically "dry" element in multimedia denies them the power and respect they deserve. How then do we craft words that work and display them in multimedia settings? How is writing for multimedia different than writing for traditional print-based media? How does it differ from writing for radio or the broadcast media?

How is it like what has come before? And how is it like nothing we've ever seen? Can technology do a better job of serving up words?

Most importantly, what do we really want to achieve now that we have this new proven technology with which to communicate?

Words with life will have even more energy if correctly combined with multimedia. Dry or boring words will only become more lost if combined with multimedia.

You are beginning an exploration into the new nature of words—words presented via computer screen.

HOW MULTIMEDIA DEVELOPED

Possibly the first real multimedia application was the silent movie.

In the early 1900s, crowds gathered in darkened theaters to look at a screen where people gesticulated while a piano player accompanied them from the music pit. After an actor mouthed a sentence the audience would lean forward, anxiously awaiting the subsequent screen of text that explained what the actor had just said.

"Don't worry, my dear! I will save you!"

Such text drew gasps from the audience as the handsome hero dashed toward the railroad tracks to untie the hapless heroine. This use of text was dramatic and invited the audience right into the action, unlike much text in multimedia today.

When "talkies" came along, text moved into the background, only to be spoken by actors or displayed during opening and closing credits. Words were still an intimate part of the process, but for the most part, they were not viewed. They were heard.

This trend remained pretty constant throughout the development of radio, movies, and television. One notable exception was the extensive use of multimedia during World War II. Millions of people were suddenly cast in the war effort as military or civilian personnel. They had to quickly learn all kinds of things, from building airplanes and buying war bonds to maintaining national security and (on a more personal front) avoiding venereal diseases overseas. In "A Brief History of Instructional Development" Sharon A. Shrock describes this multimedia blitz:

> Part of the government's response to this urgent need was the creation and distribution of thousands of training films and other mediated learning materials. According to Saettler (1968),[3] the Division of Visual Aids for War Training within the U.S. Office of Education alone produced 457 sound motion pictures, 432 silent filmstrips, and 457 instructors' manuals between January 1941, when the division was created, and June 1945. Other agencies within the armed services produced materials as well; 16-mm projectors and filmstrip projectors were purchased and distributed by the thousands during these years. Still photographs, audio recordings, transparencies, and slides were used for instructional purposes; mediated strategies were even used to create instructional simulations.[4]

Many of these productions combined text, maps, charts, graphs, music, actors, and all kinds of visuals to get the message across. Shrock explains how "calls for professionals with formal preparation in this new designer role were forthcoming."

Plus, the movie news industry produced hundreds of newsreels that utilized text, charts, interviews, and action footage in order to keep the folks on the home front carefully informed and supportive of the war effort. These were shown at movie houses prior to the main feature.

After World War II, colleges and universities quickly realized the need for people to write content for these new instructional technologies. Audiovisual departments were established on many campuses, primarily within education departments, to teach both the technology and the instructional skills needed to produce materials for slide projectors, overhead projectors, short films, and handouts. The National Education Association even founded a Department of Audiovisual Instruction to further these aims.

These days, many college art, journalism, English, language arts, business, and education departments are working to respond to the new communications demands created by multimedia. Only recently has the presentation of text become a high priority for these programs, many of which are integrating writing for multimedia components into their curricula.

WHERE MULTIMEDIA WRITING STANDS TODAY

One of the reasons so little attention has been paid to writing for multimedia is because it was developed by people whose specialties were computer science, technology, and, later, graphic arts and animation.

As recently as the 1970s, Xerox developed the first graphical user interface, or GUI (pronounced GOO-ey), which allowed computers to display not just black type or codes, but images. This led to the evolution of colors, icons, drop-down menus, window-style displays, and all the other visual elements we have come to associate with computers.

A struggling young entrepreneur named Steve Jobs had visited the legendary Xerox PARC development facility and got to see the early GUI firsthand. In 1984, he and friend Steve Wozniak introduced to the world the first personal computer that really took advantage of everything the GUI had to offer consumers. Called the Macintosh, it was the first commercially successful desktop computer and operating system. It made them multimillionaires.

After Tim Berners-Lee—nicknamed the "Father of the World Wide Web"—introduced the earliest hypertext markup language (HTML) and browser concepts, Marc Andreessen, a researcher at the University of Illinois, developed Mosaic in 1992. It was the first GUI that could read HTML, and it became the first widely used browser.

He and James Clark, founder of Silicon Graphics, launched Netscape in 1994. It was modeled on Mosaic and instantly brought the Internet to the masses. Now average people could read and create content for that part of the Internet called the World Wide Web. Netscape catapulted words into a whole new expressive realm.

Unfortunately, at least until recently, the pictures got a lot more attention than the words. Even today, there are just a few default fonts provided for Websites. But words will take on more emphasis as people continue to realize that communicating well with technology is just as important as making images look good on a screen. Words aren't just for paper anymore.

Serious studies about how people read text on-screen are finally being done. Two pioneers in this field of study are John Morkes and Jakob Nielsen.

Nielsen is a user advocate and principal of the Nielsen Norman Group, which he cofounded with Dr. Donald A. Norman (former VP of research at Apple Computer). Until 1998, Nielsen was a Sun Microsystems Distinguished Engineer.

Nielsen became very interested in how people use technology and developed a reputation as an international expert in "usability" issues. He published one critical study in the area of writing for multimedia on October 1, 1997. In "How Users Read on the Web," Nielsen concluded that

> They don't. People rarely read Web pages word by word; instead, they scan the page, picking out individual words and sentences. In a recent study John Morkes and I found that 79 percent of our test users always scanned any new page they came across; only 16 percent read word-by-word.[5]

This study was very exciting for multimedia writers like me because it gave us important insights and validated the need for our industry to pay attention to text. It was a great boost to those of us trying to convince our computer/graphics-oriented colleagues that the presentation of content was a crucial component and that it was not the same as presenting text on paper.

The results of Nielsen and Morkes's study set valid standards and gave credence to the craft of multimedia writing. While the study focused on Websites, it offered many findings that can be adapted to any on-screen presentation. Among other observations, Nielsen stated that

> Web pages have to employ scannable text, using
>
> - highlighted keywords (hypertext links serve as one form of highlighting; typeface variations and color are others)
> - meaningful sub-headings (not "clever" ones)
> - bulleted lists
> - one idea per paragraph (users will skip over any additional ideas if they are not caught by the first few words in the paragraph)
> - the inverted pyramid style, starting with the conclusion
> - half the word count (or less) than conventional writing[6]

I will be elaborating on all these points in upcoming chapters, as well as one other significant finding of the study: the importance of credibility and authenticity. Nielsen explains the significance of a credible Web presentation:

> We found that credibility is important for Web users, since it is unclear who is behind information on the Web and whether a page can be trusted. Credibility can be increased by high-quality graphics, good writing, and use of outbound hypertext links. Links to other sites show that the authors have done their homework and are not afraid to let readers visit other sites.
>
> Users detested "marketese"; the promotional writing style with boastful subjective claims ("hottest ever") that currently is prevalent on the Web. Web users are busy: they want to get the straight facts. Also, credibility suffers when users clearly see that the site exaggerates.[7]

The new technology requires a heuristic combination of traditional print-based writing and values with those of broadcast. Language must be presented visually but not superficially. Words must have both brightness and depth, energy and reflection.

Text will emerge in whole new ways, provided we urge our minds and our technologies to do more with it than has ever been done before. We have to provide multimedia content training. We have to teach ourselves to view multimedia writing as a new form of writing—one with power and potential that deserves attention and respect.

In *English for Careers: Business, Professional, and Technical*, one of the first business education textbooks to specifically address the subject of writing for multimedia in the business world, Leila R. Smith explains this unique form of communication:

> A business professional needs a wide variety of solid communication skills to deal with the multimedia of current and future technology. For the best career opportunities, acquire the language modes suited for various media. For example, each form of spoken English on the job—such as in-person, telephone conversation, or speaker's platform—requires different skills. Each type of written communication (reports, letters, interoffice memorandums, etc.) also has its own writing style. In addition, how a document will be delivered affects how it should be written; for example, mail, fax, hand-delivered, etc.
>
> In view of the varied writing styles and delivery methods for business communications, it's clear that information to be viewed on screen (whether e-mail or website) requires still other techniques. However, electronic communication also enables a live audience to view information on a screen while listening to a live presenter's comments. For a live audience, businesspeople require additional writing and speaking skills. These include deciding the number and type of words to be read and heard by the viewer for maximum effectiveness; arranging the words for quick, easy reading; and selecting the best font sizes, colors, styles, sound, movement, and anything else that impacts viewers.

Viewing and listening to multimedia presentations clearly differ from other forms of reading and listening. Therefore, business professionals need specific instruction to acquire the most effective techniques for the latest media used in business.[8]

With so many business presentations and Websites being created and maintained these days, the business world must address its ability to present content effectively in this new communications arena. Even rules regarding professional e-mails are still being refined. I, for one, always recommend using a formal salutation and complimentary close just so we remind ourselves that a business e-mail is more formal than one to Cousin Sue. Business e-mail messages can be forwarded, subpoenaed, filed on the company's server, and made more accessible to more people more quickly than any print-based correspondence. Therefore, we must be conscious of all the words we write for the screen because we cannot be completely sure who will see them.

Writing on paper is generally for a limited audience. But writing for the computer screen encompasses a broader audience, sometimes even a worldwide audience as in the case of a Website. That's why knowing how to write for multimedia is so important.

THE FUTURE OF MULTIMEDIA WRITING

Every time you use your mute button to silence the television set, you are contributing to the evolution of multimedia writing. It didn't take long for TV newsrooms and advertisers to realize that their words weren't being heard; the mute button is the enemy of the spoken word. So you'll notice today that more commercials and television shows put words on the screen. If you aren't going to listen to the message, then perhaps you'll read it. That's one reason news channels now run text in a "ticker tape" fashion across the bottom of the screen. It's also why more and more channels plant their logos in the lower right-hand corner of the screen. They want you to view the words. These are examples of how multimedia writing continues to evolve.

Exploration

Watch six television commercials.

Write down all the words they put on the screen.

Consider the words they chose to display, and decide why you think these words were selected. Discuss your opinions in class or write them for your instructor.

I keep hearing how broadband will change everything. It will make Websites flow like TV shows. It will make streaming video really stream. Some say it will turn the Internet into television and vice versa.

For writers, it will require scriptwriting and multimedia writing skills. Many more words will be seen and not heard on-screen, as well as heard but not seen. The key will be to seamlessly blend on-screen text with spoken (or voice-over) text and narrative dialogue.

Words will be more important than ever. Whether writers are creating content for a business or journalism Website, they will need to have an understanding of how to create and blend dialogue, on-screen text, and voice-over narratives. These writers will be key to the production of Websites, on-screen presentations, CD-ROMs, commercials, and other on-air segments. Their words will be utilized in multiple ways per segment, presentation, or production.

Where will people go for this kind of integrated authorship training? Forward-thinking English, language arts, journalism, broadcasting, educational technology, art, and business departments are offering courses now to meet this emerging need.

The sad fact is that for far too long, the World Wide Web has been inaccessible to writers who did not know hypertext markup language or have Web design training. But that is now changing for those who just want to write and have their words seen by the thousands upon thousands of people who use the Web. If you'd like to share your brilliant business treatise, inspire the masses with your political insight, or unveil the first chapter of your yet undiscovered novel—guess what, you can! You don't have to know anything about HTML or Web design.

The Web is finally beginning to serve writers, rather than writers having to serve the Web. This is happening in two ways:

1. Blogging
2. Direct publishing Websites

Blogging

"And now for something completely different . . ." —Monty Python
Blog sites are Websites where you register as a member (usually free), type, hit an upload button, and your work is immediately published for all the world to see. Blogging is being heralded not only by writers, but by businesses that find it a good way to build a more personal relationship with employees and customers. It's like maintaining a diary, a novella, or an ongoing correspondence with the public.

> *"There is a sense that blogging is about to explode in the business area, but who's brave enough to do it yet?"*[9]
> —Halley Suitt

> "In many cases, it is the intimate person-to-person nature of a blog that helps establish and maintain a relationship with an existing or potential customer. For many small businesses a personal relationship is their main difference from a 'faceless' large organization."
>
> —Dan Bricklin[10]

Admittedly, some blog sites are simpler to use than others. Some blogs are cheaper than others. Some are easier to read. Unfortunately, because this is an outlet geared to writers, many sites are still pretending that the computer screen displays text in the same way as paper. So the type is often too small and the layout too linear. But at least high-quality content can finally get published on the Web by writers themselves. To see how blogging works, visit

About Blogger new.blogger.com/about.pyra

About Six Apart www.sixapart.com/about

Movable Type www.movabletype.org

Direct Publishing Websites

The second new development is "online content marketplaces" where people can post writing, set prices for their work, and hopefully get discovered by a traditional publisher or by a devoted herd of Internet readers (who pay for access to the writer's content online).

It's rather like an auction site for writing—both writers and buyers use the site to reach one another. Two such new ventures are RedPepper.com and Lulu.com. These businesses encourage writers to set up shop and sell their novellas, short stories, or secret ways to stay forever young. They may charge the writers for various services, and the writers then charge the public for access.

Whether or not these Internet writing outlets build a long-term successful business model remains to be seen. But these innovations prove that writing for its own sake is now being valued on the Web.

Review

1. Multimedia presentations are outputted to a screen rather than to paper.
2. The personal computer has made the development and implementation of multimedia content a booming reality.
3. Multimedia communications generally involve three basic elements: information (content or text), visuals, and interactivity.
4. For Web developers, teachers, and business and communications professionals, understanding how to craft text for the computer screen is now required.

5. Serious attention must be paid to content basics, not just to layout, animation, images, graphics, and the other technological toys of the new computer universe.
6. Viewing words as the automatically "dry" element in multimedia denies them the power and respect they deserve.
7. One of the reasons so little attention has been paid to writing for multimedia is because it was developed by people who specialize in computer science, technology, and, later, graphic arts and animation.
8. The new technology requires a heuristic combination of traditional print-based writing and values with those of broadcast. Language must be presented visually but not superficially. Words must have both brightness and depth, energy and reflection.

Key Terms and Concepts

ARPANET   The original Internet, founded in conjunction with the U.S. military and university research departments in the late 1960s.

Copy   Words, text, or other written content.

Graphical user interface GUI   Pronounced gooey GUIs allow us to see visuals on the Internet rather than just text.

Hypertext Clickable links from one section to another, generally delineated with an underline and color different from the rest of the text.

Hypertext markup language (HTML)   The primary coding language used by anyone writing a Website for the Internet. XML is a newer HTML-like language.

Images   Photographs or graphics.

Multimedia   Any presentation combining copy, images, sound, motion, and usually hypertext. Output is to a computer screen rather than to paper.

Chapter Questions

1. How did World War II affect the development of multimedia?
2. Who were three key people in the development of computers and the World Wide Web? What did each of them contribute?

Now You Try

On the CD-ROM, visit the recommended Helpful Websites for chapter 1 to find:

- A history of the Internet
- Research about writing for the Web
- Articles on the future of Internet publishing and technology
- Blogs for businesspeople, journalists, and writers

Write 15 interesting facts you learned from visiting these Websites. Identify where each fact came from (by Website title and Web page address).

Unconventional Wisdom

- Multimedia writing combines words with sound, color, movement, graphics, and interactivity.
- A writer is also known as a content provider.
- Just because 10- or 12-point type works well in print doesn't mean it works well on the Web.
- Words deserve as much time and respect as design.

Endnotes

1. Tubbs, S. L., & Moss, S. (1994). *Human communication* (7th ed.). New York: McGraw-Hill.
2. Jonassen, D. H., & Land, S. M. (2000). *Theoretical foundations of learning environments*. Mahwah, NJ: Lawrence Erlbaum Associates.
3. Saettler, P. (1968). *A history of instructional technology*. New York: McGraw-Hill.
4. Shrock, S. A. (1991). A brief history of instructional development. In G. J. Anglin, *Instructional technology: Past, present, and future*. Westport, CT: Libraries Unlimited.
5. Nielsen, J. (1997, October). How users read on the Web. *Alertbox* [Online]. www.useit.com/alertbox/9710a.html
6. Ibid.
7. Ibid.
8. Interview with author.

9. Halley Suitt, quoted by Weidlich, Thom. The Corporate Blog Is Catching On. *New York Times*, June 22, 2003.

10. Bricklin, Dan. Small Business Blogging. *Dan Bricklin's Log*, August 12, 2002.

Answers for Chapter 1

Chapter Questions

1. *How did World War II affect the development of multimedia?*

Millions of people were suddenly cast in the war effort as military or civilian personnel. They had to quickly learn all kinds of things, from building airplanes and buying war bonds to maintaining national security and (on a more personal front) avoiding venereal diseases overseas. In "A Brief History of Instructional Development" Sharon A. Shrock describes this multimedia blitz:

> Part of the government's response to this urgent need was the creation and distribution of thousands of training films and other mediated learning materials. According to Saettler (1968), the Division of Visual Aids for War Training within the U.S. Office of Education alone produced 457 sound motion pictures, 432 silent filmstrips, and 457 instructors' manuals between January 1941, when the division was created, and June 1945. Other agencies within the armed services produced materials as well; 16-mm projectors and filmstrip projectors were purchased and distributed by the thousands during these years. Still photographs, audio recordings, transparencies, and slides were used for instructional purposes; mediated strategies were even used to create instructional simulations.

Many of these productions combined text, maps, charts, graphs, music, actors, and all kinds of visuals to get the message across. Shrock explains how "calls for professionals with formal preparation in this new designer role were forthcoming."

Plus, the movie news industry produced hundreds of newsreels that utilized text, charts, interviews, and action footage in order to keep the folks on the home front carefully informed and supportive of the war effort. These were shown at movie houses prior to the main feature.

2. *Who were three key people in the development of computers and the World Wide Web? What did each of them contribute?*

Researcher Ray Tomlinson invented e-mail in the early 1970s to transmit written messages and data quickly and easily.

In 1984, Steve Jobs and Steve Wozniak introduced to the world the first personal computer that really took advantage of everything the GUI had to offer consumers. Called the Macintosh, it was the first commercially successful desktop computer and operating system.

After Tim Berners-Lee—nicknamed the "Father of the World Wide Web"—introduced the earliest hypertext markup language (HTML) and browser concepts, Marc Andreessen, a researcher at the University of Illinois, developed Mosaic in 1992. It was the first GUI that could read HTML, and it became the first widely used browser.

He and James Clark, the founder of Silicon Graphics, launched Netscape in 1994. It was modeled on Mosaic and instantly brought the Internet to the masses. Now average people could read and create content for that part of the Internet called the World Wide Web. It catapulted words into a whole new expressive realm.

Why Are Words Important?

A word is not a crystal, transparent and unchanged; it is the skin of a living thought, and may vary greatly in color and content according to the circumstances and the time in which it is used.

—Oliver Wendell Holmes, opinion,
Towne v. Eisner, 1918

OBJECTIVES

This chapter will help you learn:

- How words affect your goals and objectives
- How words affect your design
- How words affect your audience
- How to make your words memorable

Words are important because they have power. To quote writer Pearl Strachan Hurd, "Handle them carefully, for words have more power than atom bombs." Words can build or destroy relationships.

Words have the power:

To inform

To sell

To entertain

To enlighten

To uplift

To change

To inspire

Treat words with respect—or they may come back to haunt you.

Imagine a novelist delivering her manuscript to her publishing house's editor. "I'm sorry it's so dry, but it's just words," she says apologetically.

Laughable? Of course. Words are the essence of traditional print-based writing. But for some reason, at least for now, the world of multimedia communications apologizes for having "just" words. Words have to be dressed up to be good. The power of language is not, in and of itself, enough.

The reality is that you can't make boring text interesting or compelling by adding effects to it. All you get is boring text that moves. Or boring text that is a color other than black. You actually attract more attention to boring text by adding effects. It's red, but it's still boring. It swivels, but it's still boring. It flashes, but it's still boring. To use a business analogy, it's like putting lipstick on a pig.

The greatest leaders in history did not have Microsoft PowerPoint. They had words and maybe paper. If you can't inspire with words, all the special effects in the world won't help your multimedia presentation.

Accepting an Emmy Award in 2002 for his portrayal of Leo McGarry on TV's *The West Wing*, John Spencer said, "An actor is only as good as the material he gets." He was talking about *the writing*. The same can be said of Websites and other multimedia presentations. They are only as good as the material they present.

George Lucas's first *Star Wars* movie was praised for its writing. It was a huge success. His most recent *Star Wars* movies (billed as the first two episodes) made money but were frequently criticized for being more concerned with special effects than with the caliber of the script. Audiences and critics noticed an apparent shift in priorities.

Good story lines and good scripts emphasize good writing, even more than big explosions or car chase scenes. Multimedia presentations can too easily be reduced to the level of car chase movies—big on effects but small on good writing. Words, language, and communication form the basis of any multimedia endeavor.

The well-known expression "Write what you know" stems from the idea that you will write with ease and natural authority about subjects you understand. You do not need to write from a pompous, authoritative perspective, but from a conversational, sincere point of view. Language is at its most powerful when it is purely presented.

Those of us who are professional writers need to remember this. Our writing can become overblown without warning. Recently on his television show *Ebert and Roeper*, I heard *Chicago Sun-Times* movie critic Roger Ebert say that he "experiences tearing activity" at the movies, apparently to differentiate it from crying.

The ability to write well is not a mystical gift. The best writing is genuine and natural. Don't be afraid to write. Straightforward words can have great power.

When I was young, I saw a movie called *The Miracle Worker*, starring Anne Bancroft and Patty Duke. It portrayed the lives of Helen Keller, born blind and deaf, and her teacher, Annie Sullivan. The final powerful scene depicted the moment that Keller discovered words. Her whole existence was spent inside a mental black box where she was trapped, unable to communicate. She flailed through life in anger and frustration. Her teacher, Ms. Sullivan, kept trying to open her world to language by pounding symbols for letters onto Helen's hands.

One day, while putting her hands under the spigot, Helen realized that the teacher's tapping on her palm symbolized the word for water. The existence of words brought Helen into the family of humankind. That day she was handed—literally—the gift of words and communication, the most important gift we can share. (If you haven't seen the movie and have the opportunity to rent it, I highly recommend it as an inspirational testament to the freedom and power that words give all of us.)

Words are the basis of civilization, of human relationships, of every endeavor we undertake. They outlast us. They are "mightier than the sword." If we treat words without respect, we are in essence treating ourselves without respect, for our words reflect who we are and what we believe.

Words allow you to convey your message and reach your audience. Remember that you will need to revisit your presentation periodically because society, your audience, and your information are ever-changing and evolving. So are you.

If you cheapen or misuse language, you cheapen and misuse your own message and credibility. You insult the people who have given you their precious time and trust.

Consider these words spoken by twentieth-century U.S. presidents. For better or worse, the presidents who spoke these words will always be remembered for them. See how many speakers you can identify. (The answers can be found on page 34.)

- "Read my lips, no new taxes."
- "I did not have sexual relations with that woman. . . "
- "We have nothing to fear but fear itself."
- "I am not a crook."
- "Ask not what your country can do for you; ask what you can do for your country."
- "The buck stops here."

Even the most powerful leaders of the free world may find themselves remembered for key phrases rather than their overall performance in office. That's because words matter. Legacies are enhanced or denigrated by one's own words.

HOW WORDS AFFECT YOUR GOALS AND OBJECTIVES

Having an audience is a privilege. Keeping its interest and attention is the challenge. Imparting the intended message effectively is the reward.

Words are the medium available to you to state your **goals** and **objectives**.

Goals are what you hope to impart to your viewers and the subject matter you will use to achieve that objective. In determining your goals, consider:

1. The needs of your viewers
2. The context of the conditions in which they are living
3. The format needed to present your information

As important as your goals are your **objectives**. Why are you bothering? What do you hope to achieve? What are the measurable results of your efforts? How will you assess success or failure? You can base your objectives on:

1. The knowledge you want your viewers to gain
2. The feelings and attitudes you want them to develop
3. The skills you want them to acquire

The crafting and presentation of words will help you achieve your objectives.

Exploration

Joe is planning a Website to sell cars. See how he answered the following questions.

1. **What is your primary objective?** To help people buy cars.
2. **Who is your primary audience?** Potential car buyers.
3. **List what they need to remember long-term.** My Website address. The fact that they had a positive experience using my Website.
4. **What will make using your Website a positive, memorable experience?** I will give customers all the information they need in an organized, efficient, friendly, and accurate manner.
5. **How will you achieve this?** With information and a design that gets them what they need ASAP.
6. **What will that information and design look like?** (See chapter 4.)
7. **List what they need to remember short-term.** The types, locations, ratings, and prices of various cars.
8. **Does it matter if some visitors know more about your subject matter than others?** No.
9. **If the answer is yes, how do you plan to address the various levels of preexisting knowledge among your visitors?** (Not applicable.)

How would you answer these same questions in relation to your own Website? Answering these questions will help you formulate goals and objectives.

HOW WORDS AFFECT YOUR DESIGN

How many words have you got?

If you have so many words on a Web page that your viewers have to scroll and scroll to read them all, consider alternatives. If your slide presentation has more than 35 slides, you may have two slide presentations jammed into one.

If you have a lot of words, consider whether your best medium is a printed document or a multimedia presentation. If you plan to use a multimedia presentation, and you have a lot of words, find ways to break them into manageable chunks for people who must view them on a screen.

When you are deciding on a multimedia design, two questions to consider are what kind of information are you presenting, and what kind of information do viewers expect to find? If people want to find operating hours of and directions to Disneyland, they probably don't need to buy a book. More likely, they will consult the Web. If they want to read the entire works of William Shakespeare, they probably don't want to do so by viewing a computer screen. More likely, they will buy a book. As one of my students once put it, "It's hard to curl up in front of the fireplace with a computer and read *War and Peace.*"

In the course of designing your content presentation, try to decide what can be presented best via screen, what should be made available print-style for downloading as a PDF file (for more on PDFs, see Appendix A), and what may not belong on the Web at all. If the information is just too voluminous and a book better serves the purpose, don't use multimedia except to market or supplement the book. Also, sometimes the objective is to encourage people to use their own imaginations rather than rely on your visual interpretation.

The essence of any form of writing is to communicate. What counts is getting the message and content across using the most appropriate format.

Too many words can overwhelm your design. They can make a page look "too gray" or text heavy, which can be a turnoff to a user who wants to find his or her way around quickly and easily. One way to control the number of words you put on a page (especially the home page) is to determine which words your users need to hold in memory for a long time and which words will be quickly expendable once their visit to your site is over. Your audience will not and should not be expected to remember forever all the information you present. It is unnecessary and will leave viewers feeling overwhelmed and irritated.

In planning your design for any multimedia presentation, decide what information can be **short-term** (temporary) and what information you really want your viewers to hold onto **long-term** (indefinitely).

Long-term information requires that you:

1. Spend more time on it.
2. Give it more emphasis, and put it up front on the home page.

Exploration

Every document can now be presented on paper or on-screen, depending on cost and the intended audience. What would you consider to be the best way to present the following:

A 200-page corporate annual report

Ten different recipes for vegetarian main dishes

A 400-page annual budget document

Fifty color photos of and written narrative about a vanishing rain forest

An extensive interview with a corporate president

A 700-page court transcript

A first-person account of a trip around the world

A lesson on five famous U.S. Civil War battles

A news account of a daylong Senate subcommittee hearing on terrorism

In the case of Joe's car sales Website, the following information qualifies as long-term:

- We sell cars, new and used.
- This Website tells you the price, availability, location, and history of cars for sale.
- We have an excellent reputation for service and reliability.
- Our Website address is www.neatcarsforsale.com.

Short-term information requires that you:

1. Spend less time on it.
2. Link to it from the home page.

In the case of Joe's car sales Website, the following information qualifies as short-term:

- Current car data (which changes frequently).
- Background information and press releases about our company.
- Links to auto collector Websites.
- Links to other companies that sell auto insurance and related services.

All this short-term information is really only needed while the visitor is locating and buying a car. But Joe hopes his visitors will remember his Website long-term because of its purpose, features, service, and reliability. He wants them to recommend his Website to others and return when they are ready to buy another car.

Joe's words and design reflect what he hopes will be remembered long-term and utilized short-term.

HOW WORDS AFFECT YOUR AUDIENCE

Your words will have an impact on your users. This is a fact. The kind of impact your words will have is up to you. The effect of your words can be either positive or negative, and either memorable or forgettable.

One way to construct a positive experience for your users is to observe the **Five Rules**. My former journalism professor Dr. Harvey Saalberg insisted that students memorize what he considered to be the five essential rules of written communication. At any moment, he might point to a student and say, "What are the five rules?"

To this day, I try to apply the rules to everything that I write. The rules haven't let me down, and I suggest they won't let you or your audience down either. Above all, your writing should be:

1. Accurate (Are your facts reliable? Have you confirmed them with at least two sources?)
2. Concise (Are you wasting words? Can you make the same point with less verbiage?)
3. Complete (Have you left anything out that your audience really needs to know?)
4. Clear (Does your text have to be read more than once to make sense?)
5. Objective *or* persuasive (I have added the option to be persuasive. Make a choice: Are you trying to persuade viewers to your point of view, or are you trying to present them with unbiased facts? It is important to determine this so your writing maintains credibility. Persuasive text should not try to pose as objective.)

Exploration

See if you can identify the **Five Rules** at work in the statements below. In each example, decide if the second sentence is more accurate, concise, complete, clear, objective, or persuasive (A, B, C, D, E, or F) than the first one. (For instance, the answer to Number 1 is D, Clear. The first sentence leaves it unclear to whose boyfriend they were talking. The second sentence makes it clear that they were talking to Jane's boyfriend.)

Answers are on page 34.

A. Accurate	C. Complete	E. Objective
B. Concise	D. Clear	F. Persuasive

1. Jane and Sue were talking to her boyfriend.

   Jane and Sue were talking to Jane's boyfriend.
2. Bake it in the oven for one hour.

   Bake it in the oven at 325 degrees for one hour.
3. Whenever you are writing a story, it is important to know if you are writing for a certain kind of person or people and understand whom that person or people are.

   Know and understand your readers.
4. George Washington was the fifth president of the United States.

   George Washington was the first president of the United States.
5. Pete Rose is the greatest professional baseball player who ever lived.

   Pete Rose still holds the record for most career hits (4,256), most games played (3,562), most at-bats (14,053), and most singles (3,215).
6. Eat beets.

   Eating beets gives you healthy vitamin C, iron, potassium, fiber, and folic acid.

HOW TO MAKE YOUR WORDS MEMORABLE

Whether or not words are memorable depends upon:

1. Presentation
2. Audience
3. Quality

Presentation

Here are some prevalent ideas about how to help people remember information:

- Arrange the information in an organized system. It is easier to remember facts that are in some kind of order such as a list (like this one). In educational circles, the ordering, classifying, sorting, or arranging of information into manageable chunks is called chunking.
- Put new information into a context of previously known information. Build new facts upon known facts. Bridge new information to known information with a transitional statement. Provide adequate background before supplying new information. People tend to learn by associating new information with what they already know and then building on that foundation. Supply readers with a review before expecting them to take on new facts or ideas.

- Employ mnemonics, which are word plays, rhymes, acronyms, jingles, or songs that help people recall information. "Every good boy does fine" is an example of a mnemonic that helps people recall the notes on the lines of the musical staff (EGBDF). A slogan can be useful, too, although it is technically not the same thing as a mnemonic. Unfortunately, I can still remember a slogan my boss used back in 1974 to encourage employees not to pile junk on the floor of the office where I worked as a copywriter. "Boxes off the floor in '74." So I can personally attest to the fact that slogans work and sometimes outlast their usefulness.

- Use imagery that allows viewers to form a mental picture. Your pillow company's products are so soft, it's like sleeping on a cloud. Your tooth-whitening product is so effective, it makes teeth sparkle like stars.

- Design a positive metaphor. A metaphor creates an imaginary structure that leads viewers unexpectedly to new knowledge. They may enter a cave of discovery or rocket into space to explore new information. Maybe they are playing a baseball game where every correct answer moves them further around the bases.

- Suggest an analogy. How is a corporate structure like an ant community? How is a tree like an insurance company? How is a caged tiger like a thwarted opportunity?

- Provide review. Go back over new information with a summary statement.

Audience

People have various learning styles. Normally, when we create a multimedia presentation for the screen, one of the intended goals is to advance learning. Maybe we want our viewers to learn the news, or learn about a new product or service, or learn their ABCs. In any case, chances are some aspect of learning is implied.

Learning has been defined as "a change in human performance or performance potential that results from practice or other experience and endures over time." If our goal is to promote learning, we have to provide instruction through the "selection and arrangement of information, activities, approaches, and media."[1] The more effectively this is accomplished, the more likely learning can be achieved.

Part of the goal of writing for multimedia is to make sure the writing and the medium work together for the purpose of learning and instruction.

If you wanted to teach people to ride a horse, you could give them a book to read, put them on horses, or both. If they just read a book on horseback riding, they would not become expert equestrians. A book alone is not an effective medium to teach someone how to ride a horse.

Likewise, you have to ask yourself if a multimedia presentation is the best way to enlighten your intended audience. What is it about multimedia that serves your purpose well? What might not be sufficient? How will you supplement the need for additional information?

Not only must you evaluate the strengths and weaknesses of multimedia in achieving your goals, but you must also consider your viewers. Who are they, and how do they prefer to learn or receive information?

Interestingly, over the past 20 years, educational researchers have concluded that humans learn in a variety of ways. While some can learn in a traditional schoolhouse lecture-type environment, others simply do not process information well that way.

In his landmark 1983 work entitled *Frames of Mind: The Theory of Multiple Intelligences*, Harvard researcher Howard Gardner describes at least seven separate intellectual capacities. Each offers its own distinct manner of thinking and may overlap with other "intelligences." People use a combination of learning styles to perceive, process, and retain information.[2]

Here is a summary of those seven learning styles along with an eighth style, natural intelligence, which Gardner added later. See if you recognize your own personal preferences, because you will probably fashion your Website or presentation according to how *you* learn.

- *Linguistic (verbal) intelligence.* Prefers reading, writing, listening, storytelling, memorization, and language arts.
- *Logical-mathematical intelligence.* Prefers computers, arithmetic, logic, patterns, strategy, analysis, testing hypotheses, and making predictions.
- *Intrapersonal intelligence.* Prefers independence, self-awareness, privacy, individuality, self-actualization, and expressing opinions.
- *Spatial (visual) intelligence.* Prefers visual images, art, imagery, charts and graphs, and accurate descriptions.
- *Rhythmic (musical) intelligence.* Prefers singing, playing instruments, and music appreciation.
- *Interpersonal intelligence.* Prefers an environment of cooperation, group activities and games, and social interactions.
- *Kinesthetic (physical) intelligence.* Prefers hands-on and physical activities, as well as learning by doing or seeing firsthand.
- *Natural intelligence.* Prefers the outdoors or participating in activities that involve plants, animals, nature, or earth science.

In 1980, I began the Special Species Project to teach kindergarten through 12th-grade students about language arts, science, art, social stud-

Exploration

Even more than books, multimedia makes it possible to address multiple intelligences and reach many people.

What kind of activities might you incorporate into a Website to address each of the eight recognized intelligences listed below? (Some suggestions can be found on page 34, but try your own ideas first.)

- Linguistic intelligence (word-based)
- Logical-mathematical intelligence (math-based)
- Intrapersonal intelligence (self-contained)
- Spatial intelligence (illustration-based)
- Rhythmic intelligence (music-based)
- Interpersonal intelligence (social)
- Kinesthetic, or physical, intelligence (hands-on)
- Natural intelligence (relates to the outdoors)

ies, and history by using nature as a basis for study. In 1996, I took the project from print to the Web (www.specialspecies.com). By using nature as a framework for learning, teachers have been able to fashion lesson plans that teach:

- *Language arts*—Children create poems and essays about nature.
- *Science*—Children study plants, animals, and ecosystems.
- *Art*—Children draw and paint plants and animals.
- *Social studies*—Children begin recycling, composting, and other projects.
- *History*—Children learn about historical people who cared about nature such as John James Audubon and President Theodore Roosevelt.

In varying cases, students read, draw, hold animals, plant gardens, go on field trips, sing songs, have guest speakers, or participate in other activities that engage multiple intelligences. How will your Website or presentation address viewers' various learning styles?

Quality

For people to remember something, the words have to be memorable. Too often, copywriters are adept at getting attention through the use of shocking, startling, loud, and invasive methods. But the process disintegrates quickly after that. Many times, people can recall the mechanism used to get their attention, but they have no recollection of the product, service, or idea that was supposed to be the focus.

Nobody likes to be screamed at. If Internet pop-up ads are so terrific, how come people buy software to subvert them? If banner ads are so wonderful, why don't more viewers click on them? Pushing content in people's faces at the expense of their concentration risks alienation. If you respect your viewers, you will try to engage, not interrupt, them.

> "... if a site can't stay afloat via ads that don't drive its customers crazy—or via subscription fees, e-commerce, or some other means of revenue—it probably wasn't useful in the first place."[3]
> —Brad Grimes

Various forms of online advertising have met with mixed success, so much so that many content-based Websites are turning to other strategies for producing income. An article in *ComputerUser* explains these sites' options:

> Their non-ad revenue options boil down to three basic strategies:
>
> - Persuade site visitors to pay for content, through subscriptions or pay-for-use schemes.
> - Get another Web site or publication to pay for it, through syndication or cobranding.
> - Delve into e-commerce, peddling products and services directly or feeding traffic to online merchants.[4]

For writers, this means less advertising copy to write in favor of more marketing copy and what is known as "value-added" content. The term "value-added" is a multimedia phenomenon that has always amused me. It can be defined as any content that isn't trying to sell something (or the kind of content that has filled newspapers, magazines, and journals forever).

To the Web business crowd, value-added content has been seen as an afterthought or "extra" content until now. More and more, commercial Web writers will craft words for the sake of informing, educating, entertaining, enlightening, and uplifting people—not just trying to sell them things. Value-added content will be especially needed for Websites that expect people to become paying online subscribers.

"To have any chance at all," writes Phil Davies in *ComputerUser*, "subscription sites must attract an extremely loyal following by offering content and related services that can't be found anywhere else on the Net."[5] Websites will have to offer high-quality, memorable writing.

In fact (now here's a paradigm shift for you), I consider advertising the value-added content. My Special Species Website at www.specialspecies. com is both educational and commercial—a real balancing act in and of itself. If the site has a Web page on organic gardening, the advertising links to companies that sell parasitic nematodes (they may sound treacherous, but they are really garden heroes) or books on organic gardening. If the advertising doesn't directly advance the content and assist the user, it doesn't make it on that Web page. The ads must add value to the user's experience. This is tailored advertising that blends seamlessly with the content.

Teachers have actually written to say thanks for making it so easy to find educational supplies that correspond with classroom activities covered in the content on the Website. How many Website managers can say they have received fan mail for running advertising? (Recently, however, we did get one complaint from a teacher who said we needed to offer more books for sale, so we're working on that.)

The secret of success is to provide honest content written by trained writers.

Some Websites tailor content to their advertising, rather than tailoring advertising to the content. This creates murky territory in terms of the content's integrity. If a writer prepares content praising Acme's parasitic nematodes over all other brands and if the text runs next to a half-page Acme Garden Supply flashing banner ad, users could become suspicious.

If writers are allowed to independently tackle subjects while ad salespeople find appropriate products and services, the result can benefit everyone—users and advertisers. The content and the companies that advertise will both be memorable.

For a long time, newspaper supplements and regional magazines have devoted issues to various themes. The advertising departments often sell ads to correspond with each theme.

When I worked for two years as nature editor of a home and garden magazine, we geared up for our annual Gardening and Outdoors edition by preparing articles on everything from native plant gardening to the best hiking trails. Meanwhile, the advertising department was soliciting ads from garden and recreational supply companies. East was east and west was west, and never the twain did meet. Trained writers wrote honest content, and ad departments took the theme to potential advertisers. When our magazine devoted an issue to kitchen and bath remodeling, readers benefited from the ads which pointed them to local showrooms, contractors, and designers.

Unfortunately, early on commercial interests on the Web got into the habit of just throwing a mishmash of ads at users, without providing any rhyme or reason other than making ad revenues. Too many users grew accustomed to ignoring ads or getting angry at them.

When I teach beginning Internet courses at the college level, one of the first questions I am inevitably asked by students is, "How do I get rid of all the ads?" This reaction is unfortunate because targeted advertising can be the value-added content that accompanies good writing—a philosophy the magazine world has known for years. Even general-interest newspapers make some effort to funnel ads into sections of the paper where the most interested readers will find them. Car ads go into the classified or automotive sections. Funeral home ads go on the obituaries page. Ladies' undergarment ads seem to go everywhere (excuse the digression, but I'm old enough to remember when newspapers had women's sections).

The good news is that the trend of connecting content with advertising appears to be starting on the Web, and it is positive for both ad copywriters and content providers—not to mention users. In part, the trend is taking off because of affiliate programs that attempt to directly link Websites with particular advertisers. (Learn more about affiliate programs at the Webmaster-Affiliates Program Network located at www.webmaster-affiliates.net or just by searching for "affiliate programs" through a search engine.) Through this process, Websites pick appropriate advertisers, and advertisers pick appropriate Websites based on their content. It's still a fledgling industry, but it demonstrates a definite move toward more tailored advertising content. Many Websites are starting their own affiliate programs as well, so they can handpick advertisers and better serve their target audiences.

Another approach has been pioneered by the search engine Google, which presents simple text-based ads that correspond to someone's search. These ads pertain to the topic that the user is searching. Clearly differentiated as ads, they are placed at the top, righthand part of the page in green. They don't flash, spin, pop up, pop under, or take over the screen, but they do have a strong presence without being annoying.

Unlike some search engines, which secretly place advertisers' Websites at the top of the search results, Google is very up front about separating ads from general search results. But the ads are always relevant to the search topic.

Now Google offers a "matchmaking" service that will target appropriate subject text-based ads to subscribers' Websites. When viewers click on the ads, the Websites earn revenue. To find out how it works, visit Google's AdSense at www.google.com/services/. Similar services are provided by Content Sprinks at www.sprinks.com/faq/ and Overture at smallbusiness.yahoo.com/bzinfo/prod/marketserv/overture.php. You can also type "contextual advertising" into any search engine search for a list of such sites. A recent article in *The Wall Street Journal* said "many proponents hope that contextual ad programs will encourage superior content online by giving high-quality publishers a way to survive."[6]

Exploration

Go to www.google.com and search for a topic of interest. Notice the ads that appear in green on the right side of the screen. Which two ads would you be most likely to click? Why?

Review

1. You can't make boring text interesting or compelling by adding effects to it. If you can't inspire with words, all the special effects in the world won't help your multimedia presentation.
2. Words, language, and communication are the basis of any multimedia endeavor. The best writing is genuine and simple.
3. You will write with ease and natural authority about subjects you understand. You do not need to write from a pompous, authoritative perspective, but from a conversational, sincere point of view. Language is at its most powerful when it is purely presented.
4. Words are the basis of civilization, of human relationships, and of every endeavor we undertake. Words have the power to inform, sell, entertain, enlighten, uplift, change, and inspire.
5. If we treat words without respect, we are in essence treating ourselves without respect, for our words reflect who we are and what we believe.
6. If you cheapen or misuse language, you cheapen and misuse your own message and credibility. You insult the people who have given you their precious time and trust.
7. Having an audience is a privilege. Keeping its interest and attention is the challenge. Imparting the intended message effectively is the reward.
8. In the course of designing your content presentation, try to decide what can be presented best via screen, what should be made available print-style for downloading as a PDF file, and what may not belong on the Web at all.
9. The essence of any form of writing is to communicate. What counts is getting the message and content across using the most appropriate format.
10. In planning your design for any multimedia presentation, decide what information can be short-term (temporary) and what information you really want your viewers to hold onto long-term (indefinitely). Spend more time on the long-term information and less on the short-term. Present long-term information with more emphasis.

Key Terms and Concepts

Goals   What you hope to impart to your viewers and the subject matter you will use to achieve that objective.

Objectives   Based on the knowledge you want your viewers to gain, the feelings and attitudes you want them to develop, and the skills you want them to acquire.

PDF A file that can be downloaded to read offline or saved as a file. Created by Adobe Acrobat software, which offers a free PDF Reader that you can download. (See Appendix A for more information on the software program.)

Chapter Questions

1. What are the Five Rules?
2. Name Howard Gardner's eight learning styles, or "intelligences."
3. Name four techniques for making your content memorable from a presentation standpoint.

Now You Try

On the CD-ROM, visit the recommended Helpful Websites for chapter 2 to find:

- An organization that attempts to set and track trends in online advertising
- A site that describes the latest TV news and presentation theories
- Research on the most effective and memorable ways to present text
- A comparison of good and bad Websites
- Studies on how people react to Websites

Write 15 interesting facts you learned from visiting these Websites. Identify where each fact came from (by Website title and Web page address).

Unconventional Wisdom

- Just because the writing looks fancy doesn't mean it's good.
- Words are the information in the Information Age.

Endnotes

1. Newby, T., Lehman, J., Russell, J., & Stepich, P. (1996). *Instructional technology for teaching and learning.* Upper Saddle River, NJ: Prentice-Hall.
2. Gardner, Howard. (1983). "*Frames of mind: The theory of multiple intelligences.* New York: Basic Books.
3. Grimes, Brad. "Web Savvy," *PC World,* April 2002.

4. Davies, P. (2002, March). Madison Avenue freeze-out: New revenue models could be the saving grace for content sites. *ComputerUser*, 26.

5. Ibid., 30.

6. Borzo, Jeanette (2003, October 20). On point: new services promise to deliver ads to web sites that are a lot more relevant—and a lot more lucrative. *The Wall Street Journal*, R4.

Answers for Chapter 2

1. *Here are the speakers that go with the presidential quotes presented on page 20.*

   - "Read my lips, no new taxes." George Bush, Sr.
   - "I did not have sexual relations with that woman. . ." Bill Clinton
   - "We have nothing to fear but fear itself." Franklin D. Roosevelt
   - "I am not a crook." Richard Nixon
   - "Ask not what your country can do for you; ask what you can do for your country." John F. Kennedy
   - "The buck stops here." Harry S. Truman

Exploration

The following answers complete examples on page 25.

2. *The second sentence is more* **C, Complete** *than the first one.*

3. *The second sentence is more* **B, Concise** *than the first one.*

4. *The second sentence is more* **A, Accurate** *than the first one.*

5. *The second sentence is more* **E, Objective** *than the first one.*

6. *The second sentence is more* **F, Persuasive** *than the first one.*

Exploration

Below are possible answers to the exercise on page 28.

- Linguistic intelligence: text, copy
- Logical-mathematical intelligence: puzzles
- Intrapersonal intelligence: self-evaluations
- Spatial intelligence: graphics
- Rhythmic intelligence: audio

- Interpersonal intelligence: message board, chat
- Kinesthetic intelligence: games
- Natural intelligence: nature theme

Chapter Questions

1. ***What are the Five Rules?***
   Be accurate, concise, complete, clear, and objective or persuasive.

2. ***Name Howard Gardner's eight learning styles, or "intelligences."***

   - Linguistic (verbal) intelligence: word-based
   - Logical-mathematical intelligence: math-based
   - Intrapersonal intelligence: self-contained
   - Spatial (visual) intelligence: illustration-based
   - Rhythmic (musical) intelligence: music-based
   - Interpersonal intelligence: social
   - Kinesthetic (physical) intelligence: hands-on
   - Natural intelligence: relates to the outdoors

3. ***Name four techniques for making your content memorable.*** *(Here are seven possible answers.)*

   1. Arrange the information in an organized system. It is easier to remember facts that are in some kind of order such as a list (like this one).

   2. Put new information into a context of previously known information. Build new facts upon known facts. Bridge new information to known information with a transitional statement. Provide adequate background before supplying new information.

   3. Employ mnemonics, which are word plays, rhymes, acronyms, jingles, or songs that help people recall information. A slogan can be useful, too, although it is technically not the same thing as a mnemonic.

   4. Use imagery that allows viewers to form a mental picture.

   5. Design a positive metaphor. A metaphor creates an imaginary structure that leads viewers unexpectedly to new knowledge.

   6. Suggest an analogy. How is a corporate structure like an ant community? How is a tree like an insurance company? How is a caged tiger like a thwarted opportunity?

   7. Provide review. Go back over new information with a summary statement.

3

Traditional Writing vs. Multimedia Writing

Writing is not like painting where you add. It is not what you put on the canvas that the reader sees. Writing is more like a sculpture where you remove, you eliminate in order to make the work visible. Even those pages you remove somehow remain.

—Elie Wiesel[1]

OBJECTIVES

This chapter will help you learn:

- What defines traditional writing
- What defines multimedia writing
- The similarities between the two kinds of writing
- The differences between the two kinds of writing

A Future Multimedia Writer

When I was at a friend's house recently, her 5-year-old son strode up to her and said, "Mom, get me milk." She looked him straight in the eye and did nothing. "Mom," he repeated a bit more impatiently, "I said get me milk." She continued to look at him. Except for raising her eyebrows, she did not move.

At this point, her son considered what was happening and rephrased his request. "Please, Mom," he said, "may I have some milk?" Reaching toward the cupboard for a glass, she gently admonished him. "Remember son, it's not what you say but how you say it that counts."

With multimedia, it is both what you say *and* how you say it that count. The *what* is the quality of your words, and the *how* is the way your words look. Not only must you write well, but you must consider how best to showcase every word.

For writers, multimedia is unique. In print, words are seen but not heard. In broadcast, words are heard and sometimes seen. In multimedia, words are both regularly seen and heard.

In the world of print-based publishing, showcasing every word is quite relevant to print advertising or product packaging. That cereal box you pick from the grocery shelf involved elaborate design of both words and graphics. But with other forms of traditional media, the appearance of words is pretty much limited to font size, font style, and page layout. What defines a great book is not how the words look, but what message or story the words impart. The *what* (quality of the words) supersedes the *how* (the way the words look).

As he got older, my father couldn't read the small text in many books, but he used a handheld magnifying glass because the content was worth the extra effort to him. He could have refused to read a book because of its small font size, but that would have meant missing out on great material.

I don't think he would have had the same patience with a multimedia slide presentation he couldn't read from the back of an auditorium. Despite how important the message or story might have been, I suspect he would have gotten up and politely left the room. I know I have.

When I sit to view a multimedia presentation and the presenter begins by saying, "You might want to move closer so you can see," I wonder why it is necessary for the audience to accommodate the presentation, when it should be the other way around. When a presenter says, "I know this slide is a little hard to read," I ask myself, "Then why are you showing it to me? Please fix it."

Readers of books can adapt to how words look on the page. Readers can put on glasses, use a magnifier, turn on a reading light, or hold the book in a better position. They can take a break from reading by inserting a good old-fashioned bookmark.

Viewers of multimedia presentations have no such options. They can stay, squint, and feel irritated or bored. Or they might just get up and walk out.

Viewers of Websites can enlarge or lessen type size to some degree using browser options. But if they don't want to bother, they can click out of the site altogether. Chances are, within minutes they can find another Website covering similar subject matter or selling similar products. So they don't need to extend much patience to a Website that is physically demanding or annoying to read. (Interestingly, a phone survey conducted by the Pew Internet and American Life Project in 2001 found that 62 percent of adult Web users whose favorite Websites went out of business found new, similar Websites to take their place. You can access this survey at www.pewinternet. org/reports/toc.asp? Report = 48.)

Think of your own experience. What keeps you tuned into a Website or on-screen multimedia presentation? Great writing, surely. But a welcoming atmosphere for your eyes matters almost as much.

Exploration

Visit the Web, and find three Websites you really like. Write a paragraph about each Website explaining what you find appealing.

Find three Websites you don't like. Write a paragraph about each Website explaining what turns you off.

WHAT DEFINES TRADITIONAL WRITING?

When I use the term "traditional" writing—especially as it relates to journalism, language arts, education, and business—I am referring to writing for paper. In the past, most documents were prepared for people to view on paper. This included newspapers, business letters, school reports, and most other forms of written communication.

Traditional documents are created on paper to be read by readers. This allows people to hold the documents, position them comfortably in front of their eyes (which are probably looking downward), and read them at their own pace. In this type of reading environment, people control how they look at the documents. They can pace their reading speed, go back and reread sections at will, put the documents down and return to them later, and proceed chronologically from beginning to end.

Most of the time, traditional documents are printed with black ink on white paper (just like this book). The ink dots per inch used in printing are dense, so that the text resolution is extremely clear. Whether they are interoffice memos or newspaper front pages, the ink color does not really have a major impact on how the document is read.

Because the document can be held and the reader can control the pacing, it is not unusual for traditional documents to contain large paragraphs of text, long sentences, and multisyllabic words. The words are organized across the page or in neat columns. The format is linear, structured, and formally presented. Even a restaurant menu or directions for operating a hair dryer are likely to be set up along these lines. It is a nice, neat black-and-white world where the reader is in control.

WHAT DEFINES MULTIMEDIA WRITING?

Let's contrast that with writing for multimedia, which is presented on a screen and viewed by viewers. For a variety of reasons, it is harder for people to digest and retain information projected on a screen than information printed on paper.

Viewers cannot hold multimedia presentations in their hands. They cannot really position the text comfortably in front of their eyes (which are likely looking straight ahead or upward), and—in the case of slide presentations—cannot view the material at their own pace. The presenter is in control.

The number of ink dots per inch used for on-screen text presentations is much less than that for printed documents (72 dpi is typical), so the resolution is less defined. There is a greater blurring factor for words projected onto a screen.

In this type of viewing environment, people may or may not be able to easily focus or pace their reading speed. With slide presentations, they may not be able to go back and reread sections at will, or leave the content and return to it later. They have less time to view the words.

With Websites and CD-ROMs, people are apt not to view the content chronologically from beginning to end. In this type of viewing environment, large paragraphs of text, long sentences, and multisyllabic words are much harder to read and absorb. (See Table 3.1.) Words may or may not be organized in neat columns. Content comes in many colors, and it can even move and make sounds.

In Traditional Writing	For Multimedia Writing
Typical sentence *When writing, always give careful consideration to the audience for whom content is being created.*	Shorten to *Write for your audience.*
Typical words *Colossal* *Therefore*	Simplify to *Huge* *So*
Typical expression *In anticipation of*	Shorten to *Anticipating*

TABLE 3.1   Traditional versus multimedia writing.

With slide presentations, the viewer must maintain focus and concentration while the text clicks from slide to slide under the control of the presenter. With Websites, the viewer must maintain focus and concentration while scrolling or hyperlinking. For the mind's eye, it is far from the nice, neat black-and-white world of traditional documents.

So to help the viewer digest the information in this madcap world of words, the multimedia writer should shorten sentences, limit paragraph sizes, and allow extra time for viewers to see and digest larger words, complex terminologies, and concepts.

In multimedia writing, you don't have to present everything on-screen. If you are presenting a slide presentation, use each slide as a reference point. Let the slides summarize or outline your points. Read aloud to the audience using the slide presentation as a guide rather than a verbatim text document. If there is more to say or more detail is required, rely on handouts. Prepare a traditional-style print document to accompany the slides. PowerPoint even offers you a handouts option. By all means, use it!

Likewise, with a Website, if there is more to say, select a format such as PDF. Newer versions of MSWord let you create PDFs. PDF stands for Adobe's Portable Document Format, which allows you to use Adobe Acrobat to create traditional print-style documents that people can easily read and download from your Website with Adobe Acrobat Reader. It is too difficult to force the eyes to read a huge document online. It adds loading time for many people and can prove extremely irritating, especially if they don't really want or need that much detail. Adobe Acrobat Reader is a free application available on the Internet as a browser plug-in. It allows your documents to be both viewed and printed just the way you created them. Whatever you do, don't post that 300-page annual report on your Website! Offer it as a PDF file instead. Provide a nice introductory paragraph or two about the report and then give people the option to download it if they choose.

To see some examples of PDF files on the Web, visit the U.S. Social Security Administration's Website at www.ssa.gov and click on "forms." You will see an explanation of how PDF files work and where to find the Reader download. Read more about Adobe Acrobat in Appendix A.

Exploration

Using simple words is OK in multimedia. Less is more, especially in this type of writing. This does not mean that you have to sacrifice content quality, for often the best writing is the simplest. Let a *Roget's Thesaurus* facilitate (help) you! Shorten, simplify, or replace these phrases. Possible answers are on pages 52–53.

At your earliest convenience _____

A whopping increase_____

At the present time _____

In the event that_____

It is my opinion that_____

A major crisis _____

Suffered an untimely death_____

I would appreciate it if_____

What simplified words would you substitute for the following terms? Possible answers are on page 53.

Presently _____

Assemblage _____

Intoxicated _____

Commensurate _____

Unsubstantiated_____

Elucidate_____

Using phrases rather than complete sentences is OK in multimedia. Note the differences in the two slides in Figure 3.1. Which do you think would be more readable on a screen in an auditorium?

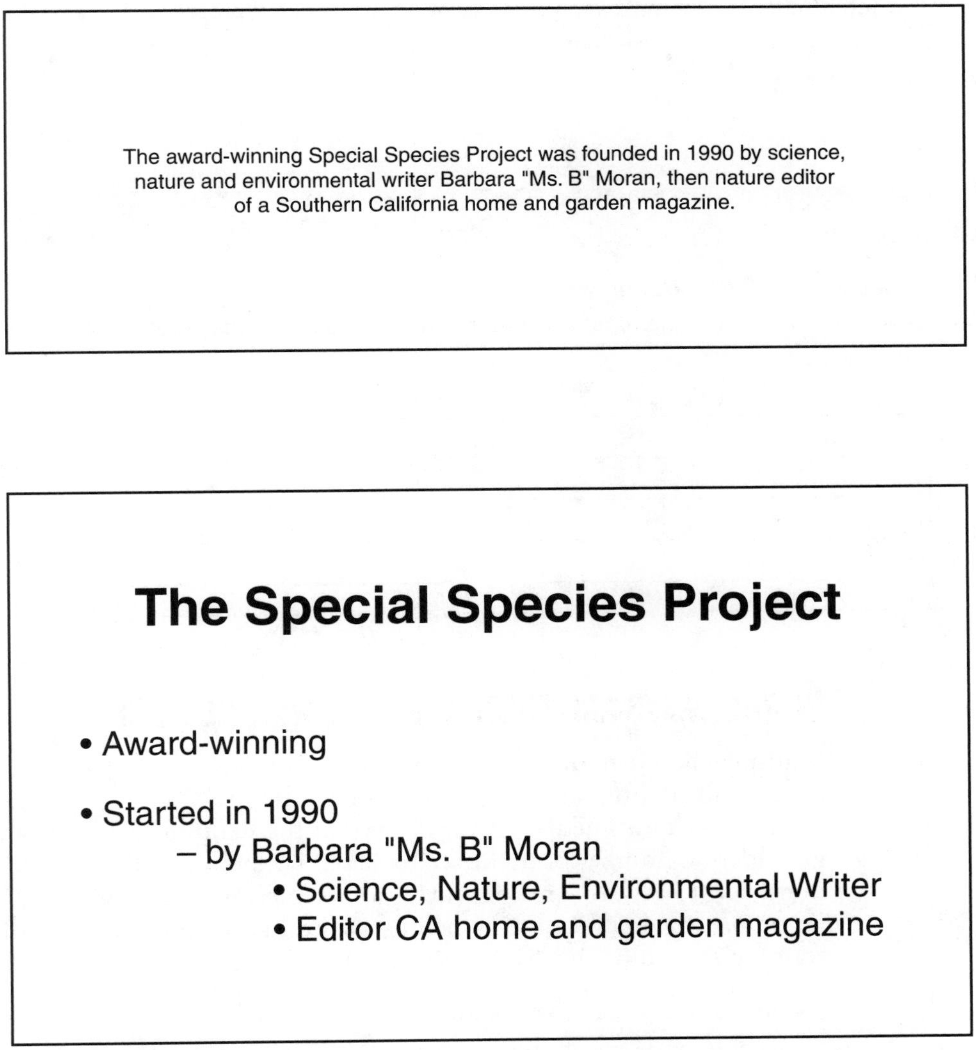

The award-winning Special Species Project was founded in 1990 by science, nature and environmental writer Barbara "Ms. B" Moran, then nature editor of a Southern California home and garden magazine.

The Special Species Project

- Award-winning

- Started in 1990
    - by Barbara "Ms. B" Moran
        - Science, Nature, Environmental Writer
        - Editor CA home and garden magazine

FIGURE 3.1 Phrases versus sentences.

Exploration

Rewrite this sentence for a slide. Use shorter sentences, phrases, bullets, and so on. A suggested answer is provided on page 53, but give it a try first.

The After-School Grant makes funds available for after-school programs and activities including tutoring, homework assistance, responsible adult supervision, and organized recreational activities.

Exploration

Using commonly understood abbreviations is OK in multimedia. Here are some commmon abbreviations. Try to identify them, and discover just how common they are! Answers can be found on page 53.

C _____   c. _____

C. _____   c _____

N.A. _____   op. _____

P.S. _____   S.A. _____

SA _____   vol. _____

IN WHAT WAYS ARE THESE TYPES OF WRITING ALIKE?

Multimedia and traditional writing both promote communication. Multimedia and traditional writing both use words.

Because multimedia writing evolved at the hands of designers and programmers, a number of traditionally based writers and editors have looked down on it—at least until recently—as an inferior form of writing. This is an unfortunate point of view because writers and editors with traditional training should be involved in this field for two reasons:

1. Multimedia is not going away.
2. People with traditional, professional training in writing and editing need to help establish the standards for multimedia writing if it is going to improve.

Whether writing is projected onto a screen, printed onto paper, or carved on stone tablets, the principles of good writing that are taught in language arts and journalism schools remain the same. The sooner writers

---

Two Views of Writing

Traditional (Letters, Newspapers, Articles, Memos, Handouts)

- Written on paper
- Read with eyes down
- Held with hands
- Seen by readers
- More time to be read
- Minimal visual impact (black type; white background; long sentences, paragraphs and columns of text)

Multimedia (PowerPoint, Web pages, etc.)

- Presented on screen
- Read with eyes level
- May not be held
- Seen by viewers
- Less time to be read
- Visual impact matters (colored type; colored backgrounds; short sentences, phrases, paragraphs or columns of words; sound and motion)

---

and editors commit themselves to learning the tools of technology, the sooner they can impact the quality of writing for the computer screen.

IN WHAT WAYS ARE THESE TYPES OF WRITING DIFFERENT?

Traditional and multimedia writing differ primarily in three ways:

1. Terminology and roles
2. Physical properties
3. Use of sources

Terminology and Roles

Since I began writing about and for multimedia in the mid-1990s, I have been called a content provider, an information designer, a project editor, an information editor, a content specialist, and a copywriter. Truth is, I'm an editor/writer. But the information technology crowd can't quite figure out how I fit into the picture unless I get some kind of tech-sounding title.

The craft of writing and editing remains the same. But a multimedia writer does function differently from a traditional author or journalist (see Table 3.2).

Traditional terms and roles	Multimedia terms and roles
Writer	Content provider
Editor	Producer or project manager (or editor)
Work with writers, graphic artists, and print production specialists	*Work with Webmasters, site designers, content providers, coproducers, or programmers*

TABLE 3.2   Traditional vs. multimedia roles.

As a writer and author, I work with an editor (or editors). Lines of communication are clear. I write, my content is edited, and off it goes to the presses without my involvement. If my story requires a graphic or photo, an artist or photographer provides one without much input from me. (Had I ever wandered down to the production room and pressroom as a writer, I would have been booted out. It may have even violated some union rule.)

But as a multimedia writer, I participate in teams. There may or may not be an editor. My content may be reviewed by a project manager who may or may not have any training in writing. I have meetings with designers and graphic artists, and we meld the content with the visuals.

To function effectively as a print journalist, I needed to know how to write. To function effectively as a multimedia journalist, I also need an understanding of graphic design, Web-authoring tools, presentation software, and computers in general.

To function effectively as a print editor, I need to know how to edit copy. I work mostly with my writers and with other editors. There is a photo editor and a graphics editor. I talk to them, and they talk to their photographers and artists.

When I work as a multimedia project editor, however, I am likely to be coordinating a team of people with various writing, design, and programming specialties. So I need management skills and a much broader understanding of the creative and outputting processes.

These requirements have precluded some very fine print-based editors and writers from entering the multimedia field, which I hope changes as more colleges begin to teach multimedia writing and editing. I went back to college in the early 1990s and took courses on my own in computers and design. There was no undergraduate department devoted to multimedia writing and editing. Now there are courses in multimedia writing and editing offered through more progressive college business, education, design, language arts, and journalism departments. But the integration between multimedia writing and traditional writing is far from accomplished. When

I visit newsrooms, I am often amazed that online editorial staffs and print editorial staffs are located on separate floors, or even in separate buildings.

Rather than synergy and collaboration, there seems to be a fear of cross-contamination. Online editions surrender the best in online design in an effort to look like printed editions. Print editions try to avoid too much writing collaboration with online editions. As the field of multimedia writing matures, I hope this mindset fades away.

The lines between writer and artist, editor and Webmaster can blur on a regular basis. I had to develop (quickly) an understanding of graphics, typography, and layout that I never needed as a daily newspaper writer. Roles are construed much differently in multimedia communications than in traditional communications.

Not only are there significant differences in the work process, but as we have seen already, there are also significant differences in traditional and multimedia writing when it comes to readers (print-based) and viewers (multimedia-based).

Physical Properties

When it comes to reading multimedia text, viewers must contend with screen glare, reduced resolution, a backlit reading surface, thousands of colors, movement, and a reading distance of 20 inches to 2 feet or more (especially if the words are projected onto a wall screen).

Reading screen content is physically stressful. On average, more than 50 percent of workers use a computer on the job, and millions suffer vision problems as a result. The condition even has its own name: computer vision syndrome (CVS). Just go to any search engine, and type in the phrase "computer vision syndrome" to see how much this has become a recognized problem. The American Optometric Association reports that about 14 percent of patients schedule eye exams specifically because of CVS.

Experts say that spending more than two hours a day working on a computer can lead to symptoms of CVS because human vision is not designed for staring at a computer screen. Computer images are made up of tiny dots called pixels. The eye can't focus on pixels, so they constantly refocus, causing repetitive stress on the eye muscles. Also, because a monitor is a moving signal, the screen is constantly being "redrawn," and the varying light intensities of red, green, and blue result in less distinct edges and lower contrast. Finally, the eyes have to use both reading and distance viewing capabilities at the same time, which can prove especially challenging for older readers.

When you are writing multimedia content, have mercy on your viewers! Give them the information they need as clearly, quickly, concisely, and completely as possible. Remember that you are not writing for paper but for

---

Computer Vision Syndrome (CVS)

Symptoms of CVS include eyestrain; fatigue; light sensitivity; blurred vision; eye irritation, such as dryness or burning; red, itchy, watery eyes; heaviness of the eyelids or forehead; difficulty focusing; and headaches, backaches, muscle spasms, and pain in the shoulders and neck.

Causes stem in part from the fact that computer users don't blink as often as those who read printed documents. They may also produce fewer tears. They have to endure glare, reflection from the monitor, reduced resolution, odd reading distances, scrolling, movements on screen, and sometimes improper glasses or bifocals (which cause the wearers to tip their heads back, increasing neck strain).

---

a medium that is very, very different. Take into account how to ease the burden on your viewers' eyes.

Again, these factors don't affect writing and editing for traditional print-based media. When I worked as a traditional journalist, type size and layout design were important, but I never worried about glare. Sometimes readers would glare at my newspaper, but it never glared back.

Use of Sources

Another difference between traditional and multimedia writing involves the use of sources. Traditional sources include books, journals, and other print-based materials, as well as interviews with people that are interpreted and transcribed by the writer. Multimedia sources also include Websites.

For some tradition-based writers, a Website must always be used cautiously as a source of information. To them, writing that appears on a screen cannot possibly have the credibility of words on paper.

Multimedia writers are more willing to cite Websites as sources. Rather than interview someone and write my interpretation of what they said, I often go directly to sources' Websites and let them speak for themselves.

In one case, for example, I was writing an online news account about renewed whaling efforts. I referred my Website's viewers directly to the sources involved. One hyperlink at the end of my story went to the Website of the Icelandic fishermen who wanted to whale again. The second hyperlink at the end of my story went directly to the Website of the environmental group opposing the idea.

Here, my mission as a multimedia writer was to set the stage and provide the background, then take my viewers directly to the Websites of the affected parties. In their own words, through their own Websites, they could make their cases directly to my viewers without my interpretation or partiality clouding the central issues.

For another story, I was writing about the Cuban shooting down of small aircraft pilots from Florida. The pilots claimed they were dropping leaflets. The Cuban government contended they were spies. At the end of my story, I linked my viewers directly to the pilot association's Website and to the Cuban government's Website, so they could evaluate each source for themselves.

This approach to multimedia reporting lessens the writer's role as middleman or interpreter. The writer becomes more of a moderator who lays the foundation and then lets the subjects speak for themselves. Unless my job is to be an online commentator or provide interpretation, this format creates a more objective forum for the parties to make their own cases.

Many sources now have their own Websites. A writer's credibility is important, but so is the right of a source to express him- or herself without the filter of a writer's point of view. If a source is making a ridiculous argument, intelligent viewers can usually figure it out.

Writers can assist their viewers by supplying an e-mail address where they can be reached for feedback. This also helps writers stay in touch with their viewers' thoughts.

Writers do need to evaluate the credibility of any Website they use as a source. For that matter, anyone who cites a Website needs to judge its quality. Here are some guidelines:

- Consider the source itself. What is its reputation for integrity and knowledge of the subject matter?
- Consider the timeliness of the information. Unlike a book, which gets written and revised every few years, a Website should be updated regularly and state how often updates are made. Daily, weekly, or monthly updates are preferred.
- Consider the proximal association. How close is the Website to the original source of the information? Is it a Website *quoting* the American Medical Association, or is it *the* Website of the American Medical Association? Firsthand information is ideal. Go directly to the primary source of the information.

And remember, when people are evaluating *your* Website, they will probably be using the same or similar criteria.

If you cite a Website as a source, and you aren't sure which style to use (various uses require various styles), here is a good all-purpose format. If available, the citation should include:

1. The Website title (in quotes)
2. The author's name
3. The date of publication
4. The title of the specific article

5. The date you accessed it

6. The URL of the exact Web page from which you took the information

If all of these elements are not available, include as many as you can. So a reference might look like this:

"All about kumquats." Smith, T. (2000, April). Health Benefits of Kumquats. Retrieved February 15, 2001, from www.allaboutkumquats. com/facts/health.htm

For more on citing sources, visit American Psychological Association (APA) style at www.apastyle.org/elecmedia.html or Modern Language Association (MLA) style at www.mla.org/style.

Remember that the purpose for which you are using the Website may impact how you cite it. If it's for a journalism or business article, the citation may be different than for a professional online journal. If in doubt, ask the editor or project manager.

Review

1. With multimedia, both what you say *and* how you say it count. The *what* is the quality of your words, and the *how* is the way your words look. Not only must you write well, but you must consider how best to showcase every word.

2. In print, words are seen but not heard. In broadcast, words are heard and sometimes seen. In multimedia, words are both regularly seen and heard.

3. What defines traditional writing is not how the words look, but what message the words impart. The *what* (quality of the words) supersedes the *how* (the way the words look).

4. The number of ink dots per inch used for on-screen text presentations is much less than that for printed documents (72 dpi is typical), so the resolution is less defined. There is a greater blurring factor for words projected onto a screen.

5. Less is more, especially in multimedia writing. This does not mean that you have to sacrifice content quality, for often the best writing is the simplest.

6. Using phrases rather than complete sentences is OK in multimedia. So is using commonly understood abbreviations.

7. If there is more to say or more detail is required, rely on handouts. Prepare a traditional-style print document to accompany any slide presentation. Likewise, with a Website, if there is more to say, use a format such as PDF.

8. Whether writing is projected onto a screen, printed onto paper, or carved on stone tablets, the principles of good writing that are taught in language arts and journalism schools remain the same.

9. Courses in multimedia writing and editing are offered through progressive college business, education, design, and journalism departments.

10. Writing and editing roles in multimedia communications are much different than in traditional communications.

11. There are also significant differences in traditional and multimedia writing when it comes to readers (print-based) and viewers (multimedia-based).

12. Viewers must contend with screen glare, reduced resolution, a backlit reading surface, thousands of colors, movement, and a reading distance of 20 inches to 2 feet or more (especially if the words are projected onto a wall screen).

13. For multimedia text, the eyes have to use both reading and distance viewing capabilities at the same time, which can prove especially challenging for older readers.

14. Another difference between traditional and multimedia writing involves the use of sources. Traditional sources include books, journals, and other print-based materials, as well as interviews with people that are interpreted and transcribed by the writer. Multimedia sources also include Websites.

15. Writers need to evaluate the credibility of any Website they use as a source. Here are some guidelines: Consider the source itself. Consider the timeliness of the information. Consider the proximal association. When people are evaluating *your* Website, they will probably be using the same or similar criteria.

Key Terms and Concepts

Multimedia writing Writing for a computer screen.

Traditional writing Writing for paper.

Chapter Questions

1. What are six differences between traditional and multimedia writing?
2. Name two ways multimedia and traditional writing are alike.
3. How are the terms and roles of traditional writing different from those of multimedia writing?
4. Name three ways to evaluate the credibility of a Website.

Now You Try

On the CD-ROM, visit the recommended Helpful Websites for chapter 3 to find:

- How e-mail newsletters differ from printed ones
- Ways to make sure your multimedia writing is clear, concise, and correct
- A nicely organized series of lessons on instructional design
- A look at using computers as vehicles for learning
- Research on cognitive science and reading

Write 15 interesting facts you learned from visiting these Websites. Identify where each fact came from (by Website title and Web page address).

Unconventional Wisdom

- Books are read line by line; Websites are viewed randomly.
- In multimedia, words may be both seen and heard.
- Print has readers; multimedia has viewers.
- Computer screens are hard on eyes.

Endnote

1. Interview in *Writers at Work*, Eighth Series (1988). Plimpton, G. (Ed.) New York: Viking.

Answers for Chapter 3

Exploration

These shortened phrases are possible answers to the exercise on page 42.

At your earliest convenience: Soon
A whopping increase: An increase
At the present time: Now
In the event that: If
It is my opinion that: I think

A major crisis: A crisis
Suffered an untimely death: Died
I would appreciate it if: Please

These simplified words are possible answers to the exercise on page 42.

Presently: Now
Assemblage: Crowd
Intoxicated: Drunk
Commensurate: Equal
Unsubstantiated: Unproven
Elucidate: Explain

Exploration

Below is one suggested answer for the exercise on page 44.

The After-School Grant funds

After-school programs

- Tutoring
  - Homework help
  - Supervision
  - Recreation

Exploration

The following are possible answers to the list of abbreviations on page 44.

C = capacitance (relates to electricity), Carbon, Celsius, centigrade,
Roman numeral for 100, a grade of third highest, a musical tone

c. = cloudy, cup

C. = Catholic, Celtic, Chancellor, Chief, City, Congress, Conservative

c = candle (in physics), carat, cubic

Note: The abbreviations above are based on whether or not the letter C is capitalized or followed by a period.

N.A. = Narcotics Anonymous, National Academician, National
Academy, North America

op. = operation, opposite, opus, out of print

P.S. = permanent secretary, police sergeant, postscript, public school

S.A. = Salvation Army, South Africa, South America, Sturmabteilung

SA = South Australia, Sexaholics Anonymous

vol. = volcano, volume, volunteer

Chapter Questions

1. ***What are six differences between traditional and multimedia writing?***

   1. Written on paper vs. presented on screen
   2. Read with eyes down vs. read with eyes level
   3. Held with hands vs. possibly not held
   4. Seen by readers vs. seen by viewers
   5. More time to be read vs. less time to be read
   6. Minimal visual impact (black type; white background; long sentences, paragraphs, and columns of text) vs. visual impact matters (colored type; colored backgrounds; short sentences, phrases, paragraphs, or columns of words; sound and motion)

2. ***Name two ways multimedia and traditional writing are alike.***

   They both promote communication, and they both use words.

3. ***How are the terms and roles of traditional writing different from those of multimedia writing?***

   - People traditionally called writers are called content providers in multimedia.
   - People traditionally called editors are called producers or project managers (or editors) in multimedia.
   - In print, editors work with writers, graphic artists, and print production specialists. In multimedia, they work with Webmasters, site designers, content providers, coproducers, or programmers.

4. ***Name three ways to evaluate the credibility of a Website.***

   1. Consider the source itself. What is its reputation for integrity and knowledge of the subject matter?
   2. Consider the timeliness of the information. Unlike a book, which gets written and revised every few years, a Website should be updated regularly and state how often updates are made. Daily, weekly, or monthly updates are preferred.
   3. Consider the proximal association. How close is the Website to the original source of the information?

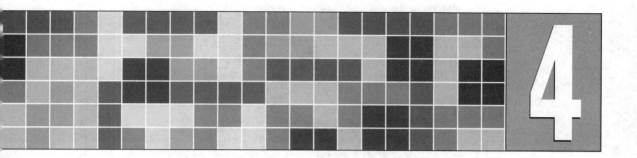

Creating Your Content

One cannot make the words too strong.

—Mark Twain[1]

OBJECTIVES

This chapter will help you learn:

- How to consider the legalities
- How to plan and organize content for a Website
- How to plan and organize content for a slide presentation

CONSIDER THE LEGALITIES

Technology has changed how we write, and it is changing copyright laws as well. Copyright seems to be in a constant state of flux, or as *The Wall Street Journal* put it, "When it comes to the issue of copyright, most people can agree on one thing: It's a mess."[2] One person's file sharing is another person's stealing. Still, there are rules to follow, particularly with regard to plagiarism.

Never forget that plagiarism is a crime, punishable in the United States by potentially huge fines. Plagiarism involves stealing the words and images conceived by another human being. To plagiarize means:

> 1. To use and pass off (the ideas or writings of another) as one's own. 2. To appropriate for use as one's own passages or ideas from (another). To put forth as original to oneself the ideas or words of another.[3]

Or, put another way, it means "to steal or purloin from the writings of another; to appropriate without due acknowledgement (the ideas or expressions of another)."[4]

You can share the words and images of other people, but only if you give them proper credit as the originators of those words and images. And your original writing, art, and photography are afforded the same rights.

If you feel tempted to plagiarize, don't believe that no one will ever find out. There are software programs today that can look for text and images and report their use back to the originator.

Respect the Work of Others

In any kind of writing, it is important to examine the source of your content. Will you be using direct quotes or information from another source, or will all content be original?

Because the world of multimedia is ever evolving, so are the rules for attribution. But suffice it to say that you must give credit where credit is due. You cannot copy and paste text from a Website or download an image without acknowledging the source in some formal fashion. For slide presentations, it is best to have a final "Resources" slide that spells out the source of any quotes or images used within your presentation. For a Website, credit the information you have used somewhere on the Web page where it is found.

If you are using content from another source or including information from someone else's Website, you may need to seek permission in writing. If you're simply linking to another site, different rules may apply. When it comes to incorporating other sources into your writing, here are some general guidelines to follow:

1. If you use anyone's text verbatim, you must give the author credit and quote the material properly. Even though the material exists in cyberspace, copyright rules apply.

2. Put textual material in quotes. If it is a short quote, you can use it without seeking permission of the author. If you are basing an entire slide presentation or Web page on someone else's work, however, it is wise to try and get written permission from the author or owner of the material.

3. At a minimum, you must cite the title of the Website, the section you used, and the Website address that includes that section. For example:

"Special Species." *Teacher's Corner—Anthropology,*
www.specialspecies.com/teacherscorner/anthropology.htm.

4. When linking to someone else's Website, be sure that your link makes it clear to visitors that they are no longer on your Website. The use of frames makes it easy to mask this, so that another Website appears to be sitting within your own, but for safety's sake, it is best to open the link in another, separate window, so viewers understand that you have led them to a different Website altogether.

5. Likewise, you must clearly acknowledge the source of any image you put on your Website or into your slide presentation unless it is copyright-free clip art. You may type the information below the image or link the image to its source of origin.

6. Keep up to date on multimedia copyright rules. One good way to do this is by visiting Yahoo's collection of Websites that deal with this subject (dir.yahoo.com/Government/Law/Intellectual_Property/Copyrights).

7. The Tech Law Journal (www.techlawjournal.com) is devoted to "legal, legislative, and regulatory issues affecting the computer, Internet, information, and communications industries." Late-breaking developments in the copyrights area are reported here. You can also find current information at ZDNet (www.zdnet.com). Key the word *copyrights* into the search box to find the latest articles on this topic as it relates to cyberspace and multimedia.

There are "fair use" provisions that allow you to use another's material for personal, educational, and noncommercial reasons. These provide a bit more flexibility than if you are using someone else's images or text to make money for yourself. According to the Library of Congress's Copyright Office,

> One of the rights accorded to the owner of copyright is the right to reproduce or to authorize others to reproduce the work in copies or phonorecords. This right is subject to certain limitations found in sections 107 through 118 of the copyright act (title 17, U.S. Code). One of the more important limitations is the doctrine of "fair use." Although fair use was not mentioned in the previous copyright law, the doctrine has developed through a substantial number of court decisions over the years.[5]

Codified in section 107 of the copyright law, some of the potentially acceptable fair uses are

> criticism, comment, news reporting, teaching, scholarship, and research. Section 107 also sets out four factors to be considered in determining whether or not a particular use is fair:
>
> 1. the purpose and character of the use, including whether such use is of commercial nature or is for nonprofit educational purposes;
> 2. the nature of the copyrighted work;
> 3. the amount and substantiality of the portion used in relation to the copyrighted work as a whole; and
> 4. the effect of the use upon the potential market for or value of the copyrighted work.[6]

The Copyright Office acknowledges that the line between "fair use" and copyright infringement may not always be clear. There are no specific rules related to how much can "safely be taken without permission." And just stating the source of the copyrighted material is no substitute for obtaining written permission.

In the past, courts have upheld the use of another's material as "fair use" in relation to

> quotation of excerpts in a review or criticism for purposes of illustration or comment; quotation of short passages in a scholarly or technical work, for illustration or clarification of the author's observations; use in a parody of

some of the content of the work parodied; summary of an address or article, with brief quotations, in a news report; reproduction by a library of a portion of a work to replace part of a damaged copy; reproduction by a teacher or student of a small part of a work to illustrate a lesson; reproduction of a work in legislative or judicial proceedings or reports; incidental and fortuitous reproduction, in a newsreel or broadcast, of a work located in the scene of an event being reported.[7]

But the Copyright Office stresses that getting permission is always the safest avenue. "When it is impracticable to obtain permission, use of copyrighted material should be avoided unless the doctrine of 'fair use' would clearly apply to the situation. The Copyright Office can neither determine if a certain use may be considered 'fair' nor advise on possible copyright violations. If there is any doubt, it is advisable to consult an attorney."[8]

You may obtain a downloadable PDF version of the fair use doctrine by visiting the Library of Congress at www.loc.gov/copyright/fls/fl102.pdf or by writing to the Copyright Office at 101 Independence Avenue S.E., Washington, D.C., 20559-6000.

Protect Your Own Hard Work

You have the right to copyright any multimedia work you create to protect your *own* content from being plagiarized. The Copyright Office gets more than 500,000 applications each year.

Just because your document appears on a computer screen rather than on paper does not make it any less legitimate in the eyes of the law. You can copyright the content and images on your Website or in your slide presentation. Start by inserting this format on any Web page or at the beginning of a slide presentation:

Copyright © (year created) by (name of owner—individual or company)

So it might look like this:

Copyright ©2003 by Barbara Moran

Under current law, the copyright in a work is initially owned by the work's creator, but this isn't always the case (for example, if you are writing under a "work for hire" contract, or if you create a work as an employee in the course of your employment, in which case your employer owns the copyright). Anything else you create from your own brain using your own words automatically belongs to you—usually.

To strengthen your copyright protection, you may wish to file an official application with the Copyright Office. Forms can be downloaded from the U.S. Copyright Office Website at www.loc.gov/copyright. (You need

Adobe Acrobat Reader installed on your computer to view and print the forms, but it's free and you can download it at the Copyright Office Website. Follow carefully the instruction provided in terms of how to prepare the forms, or they will be returned to you unprocessed.)

To ensure that your application is received, send it registered or certified mail and request a return receipt. Once your forms are submitted, it takes about eight months to have them processed. During this time, a Copyright Office staff member may contact you by letter or phone if more information is needed. If your application is approved, you will get a certificate of registration to confirm that your work has been registered. If it is not accepted, you will get a letter explaining why it was rejected.

Additional information from the Copyright Office about current rules and regulations is also available at the Website. Or you may call (202) 707-2600 to request information—not forms—via fax (you must use a Touch-Tone phone). For further information, send a letter to Library of Congress, Copyright Office, Information Section, LM-401, 101 Independence Avenue S.E., Washington, D.C. 20559-6000.

If you need additional application forms for copyright registration, call the Copyright Office Forms and Publications Hotline at (202) 707-9100, and you will get a recorded message to leave your request. To speak to an actual live person who can address your questions or needs, call (202) 707-3000, TTY (202) 707-6737.

Finally, if you want to ensure protection of your work, mail copies of the work to yourself on disk or CD-ROM. Don't open the envelopes when they arrive. They will have the postmark on them, which will serve to show the time at which you mailed them to yourself. That way, if anyone claims to have created your work, you can take the sealed envelopes to court and ask a judge to open them. The postmark will predate any effort by a plagiarist to claim your work as his or her own.

Getting Started

Writing for publication—multimedia or print—is basically a three-step process. First you have to gather and *process* in your own mind any information you plan to use. Then you have to determine a way to *organize* the information into a coherent structure. Finally, you need to *present* the information in the most effective manner.

Go POP!

Process Information

Organize Information

Present Information

Why are you building a Website or writing a presentation? Sometimes *why* is the hardest question to answer. Complete this exercise to help you find out *why*.

1. Fashion a question based on the following choices: What (choose one) **subject, idea, product, object, concept, value, belief, point-of-view, perception, event, skill,** or **service** am I trying to (choose one) **sell, impart, provide,** or **explain?**

2. Write a statement in answer to the question you just fashioned. [For example: The **subject** I am trying to **explain** is (insert your answer here). The **product** I am trying to **sell** is (insert your answer here). The **service** I am trying to **provide** is (insert your answer here).]

PLAN AND ORGANIZE CONTENT FOR A WEBSITE

When you visit someone's home, chances are they greet you at the door and warmly welcome you inside. They show you around and help you feel at home. This is how viewers of your Website should feel as soon as they arrive. You show them around immediately to help them feel at home.

It is important to remember during this initial process that you are not really concerned with the graphic design at this point. The color and shape of the buttons, the appearance of your background, and so on are questions for the design phase of your Website.

Right now your objective is to decide your content needs and how to organize content within your Website. This step should happen before you even begin to think about colors, images, and other graphic design elements.

Before proceeding further, I'd like to review some Web terminology:

Address: This is the uniform resource locator (URL) for your Website, such as www.specialspecies.com. The part of this address that says "special-species" is the domain name that you establish. You think up what you want this part of your address to be; then you apply for it as a domain name.

Home page: The first page or introductory page of a Website.

Web page: Any single page of a Website.

Website: The entire collection of Web pages and the home page.

Think of your Website as an electronic book. The home page contains the table of contents, or navigation bar in Web lingo. Your navigation bar tells viewers what all your Web pages contain.

Exploration

If you have a party, you want people to come. You may send out invitations. When you put up a Website, you also want people to come. Here is an imaginary invitation to get people to visit your Website. Complete these sentences with your own answers of any length.

Dear potential viewers:

I created this Website because I believe it will . . .

My Website is of value to you. It will help you . . .

After viewing my Website, you will be able to . . .

Your feedback is important. Here's how to contact me to offer your input and ideas . . .

Each Web page is a chapter in your electronic book. But unlike a traditional book, people will not read your pages in order. They may read the last page first. So all your pages need to connect with one another as well as stand alone. And all of them should lead your viewers back to your home page. This can be accomplished by making sure there is a "Home" button on every page.

The home page is the first page to plan. The current trend is to have a home page that requires no scrolling. Everything a viewer needs to find out about your Website is contained "over the fold" (newspaper slang meaning on the upper half of the page). In this case, there is no scroll bar on the home page.

The following content areas need to appear on your home page. I call these the Four Essentials:

1. *Title*—What is the title of your Website? Like a book, your Website needs a title. Once you have decided on a title for your Website, search for it on the Internet (using several different search engines) to make sure it hasn't already been taken. You want a title that is clear and not in use by anyone else. If the Website is for a company, it may just be the company's name (for example the "Go Native" Plant Nursery and Design Company). Or you may want a title that reflects the mission of the Website (for example, Save Endangered Plants).

Again, it is a good idea first to look at Websites with the same or a similar mission or product as yours. Once you come up with an idea, make sure another Website isn't already using it. You can do this by searching with search engines or hiring an attorney to search for you.

The final step is to apply for a domain name if you want your Web address to reflect your Website's title. Having a Website address that contains the words of your Website title makes it easier for people to remember. For example, CNN's Website address is CNN.com.

To apply for a domain name, contact the company that will be hosting, or displaying, your Website. Or use a company such as Network Solutions (www.networksolutions.com), which has a long, reliable track record. There are fees, both for registering and then for maintaining your name.

2. *Table of contents (navigation bar)*—What buttons or words will you use to direct viewers to all the other pages on your Website? (For example, buttons might include "Buy Pet Supplies," "See Student Projects," "Try Fun Experiments.")

3. *Blurb*—The blurb is a phrase, sentence, or short paragraph that tells viewers the purpose of your Website. It can be a phrase ("*the* place to buy kumquats"), a sentence ("We're the bank you can trust."), or a paragraph ("Welcome to the project-based learning adventure for teachers and students! See what happens when teachers, nature advisers, and kids explore plants, animals, and habitats together.").

4. *Introduction (or lead-in)*—This tells viewers where to start. It helps them get acclimated and begin using your Website. It may be the largest headline on the page. It may also be a secondary set of navigational words. It can be a button, phrase, or sentence (for example "Giant Kumquat Sale!" or "Class Play Auditions Begin This Week."). But it clearly tells viewers, "Begin here" and entices them into your Website.

Of course, you will also need graphic and design elements, but we are going to focus primarily on the writing. Organizing the textual elements helps determine the best mood, look, and design for the whole Website. It needs to be the first step in Website design rather than the last.

Exploration

1. Go on the Internet and research "how to apply for a domain name." Write two paragraphs on what you learn. Using a search engine such as Google (www.google.com), you may also wish to search the following terms: "Verisign," "Network Solutions," "InterNic," and "Internet Society."

2. Using three different search engines, insert the title of your proposed Website into the search box and see if any other Websites exist with the same or similar titles.

Exploration

On the accompanying CD-ROM, click on www.specialspecies.com to access the home page. You may also refer to Figure 4.1. Identify the following:

1. Title—What is the name of the Website?
2. Table of contents (navigation bar)—What buttons or words direct viewers to all the other pages on the Website?
3. Blurb—What phrase, sentence, or short paragraph tells viewers the purpose of the Website?
4. Introduction (or lead headline)—What helps viewers get started? What suggests that viewers "begin here"?

Does this home page do a good job of presenting the four basic elements? Why or why not? Do you have suggestions for improvement? Write or discuss your opinions.
Do this same exercise five times using five Websites you find on the Internet.

Deciding on your title, table of contents, blurb, and introduction will go a long way toward helping you envision your entire Website. It helps you focus on the content and solidify what you want to achieve.

Even if you already have a Website, going through this exercise can help you evaluate how efficiently your home page is built. Try to eliminate the need for scrolling, which is now considered old-fashioned on a home page.

Exploration

Complete the following form.

The title of my Website will be:

My table of contents (navigation bar) will have these four to six topics:

1.
2.
3.
4.
5.
6.

My blurb will say:

My introduction (or lead-in) will say:

My lead headline will say:

FIGURE 4.1   Specialspecies.com home page.

Once you have decided on the Four Essentials of your home page, you can draw a mock-up of the page. See Figure 4.2 for an example. If you know how to use the Web page option in Microsoft Word, or if you are familiar with Web design software, that's great. You can use a slide in PowerPoint as a mock-up space. But you can also take a piece of typing paper and turn it sideways, so that it is wider than it is long. (Computer screens display content in this way.)

Exploration

Draw out your concept for your home page on a piece of typing paper turned sideways. Place the Four Essentials where you think they should be. Leave a space for a graphic. Write all your text on the paper where it would appear. Don't worry too much about formatting and design right now. The important thing is to plan all the words.

A finished drawing or PowerPoint rendition might look something like the example in Figure 4.2.

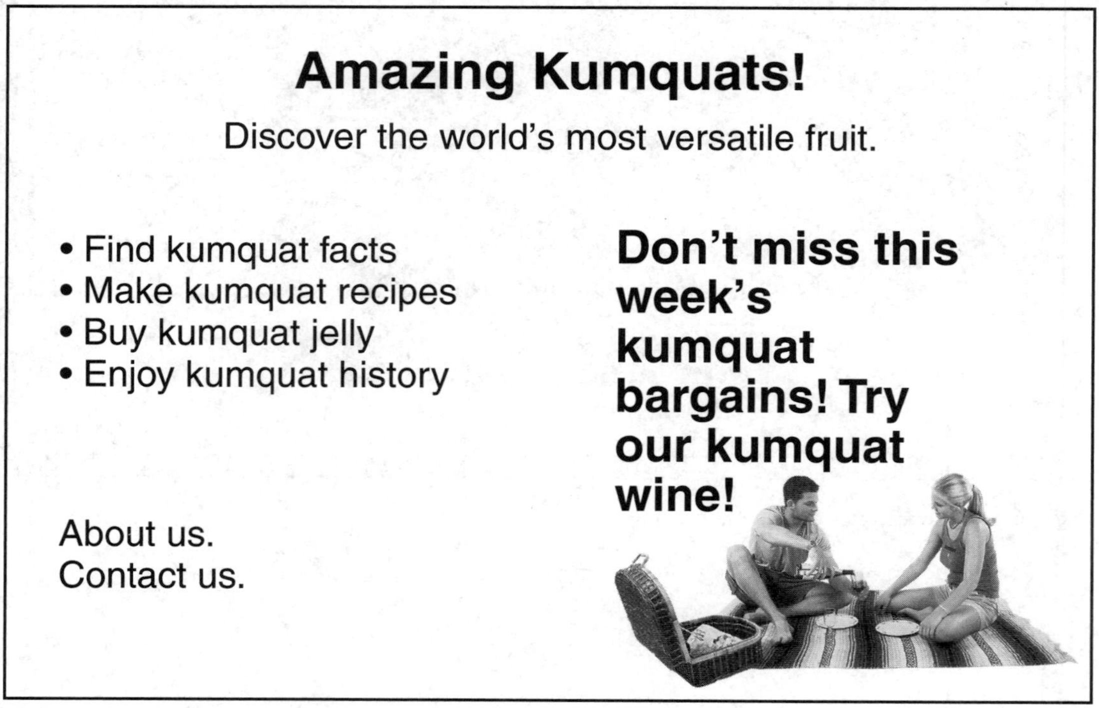

Amazing Kumquats!

Discover the world's most versatile fruit.

- Find kumquat facts
- Make kumquat recipes
- Buy kumquat jelly
- Enjoy kumquat history

Don't miss this week's kumquat bargains! Try our kumquat wine!

About us.
Contact us.

FIGURE 4.2 Example of home page mock-up.

Once you have decided what will be on your navigation bar, you can envision additional Web pages. Every link on your navigation bar should take viewers to a unique Web page with the same basic title as the button on the navigation bar.

Now you can write content for each of those Web pages. Don't worry about formatting or design. Settle instead on what the words will be. Build a first draft of content for each page.

Remember, the great thing about multimedia is that it can always be changed, modified, and added to or subtracted from—so these are working documents. Unlike a book, which is permanent once it has been committed to ink, your Web pages can be easily edited as the process of Web building continues.

Preparing your content first helps designers envision what you want to say and how best to present it visually. If you are your own designer, the same principle holds true. Should you have a lot of content for any one section, you can see how you may need to break it into more than one Web page. What will remain on your top-level page? What content could you put on a secondary page? Feel free to cut and paste your text onto additional pieces of typing paper if it helps you visualize the "layers" of content you are building. You are creating a working outline of a Website.

Remember that each Web page must connect with others, so decide what buttons you need to link people to the beginning and back up the chain of layers you may create.

In essence, you are constructing a content inventory for each Web page. As you make this inventory, consider the following questions: What topics do you plan to address, what are the specifics you will cover under each topic, and in what order will you present them? What can go deeper into your site, and what needs to stay near the top (on the home page or first linking page). A rule of thumb is that the closer you are to the home page, the fewer words you should use. As you go deeper into the Website, you can create pages with more words. If I need to include a large document, I seldom put it on the Web page, but instead I create a PDF document that people can download and read off-line. Or I create an HTML version that loads into a separate window from the Web page. (On the CD-ROM that accompanies this book is a process you can use to begin writing content for each level of your Website.)

Try this trick when drafting content for a Website.

Use 16-point type for home page content.
Use 14-point type for second-level pages.
Use 12-point type for third-level pages and beyond.

You will want to build new, complex information on the foundation of the simplest information. Start with the simplest information first. This provides needed background and a mental "staging area" for your viewers, as you introduce them to more complex ideas and data. People learn by building upon existing knowledge.

If viewers have no idea what broadband is or what DSL stands for, they probably won't be too receptive to a Website that's trying to sell them a DSL connection. The top level of the Website needs to provide enough explanation to "hook" viewers by confirming what they already know and then making them want to learn more. For example, you might write something such as:

> On the Internet? Are you crawling at modem speed, or would you like to fly at DSL speed? For just a little more money each month, you can turn your computer trolley into a bullet train using our DSL service! It's easy and reliable. Blast off right now.

If your site is selling virus-protection software, but viewers aren't sure what a virus is, they probably won't be drawn in by your sales pitch. You can pretty well assume that your viewers know what a computer is! But make sure you explain potentially new terms and ideas if you hope to build interest from there. Terms can go into a separate box, for example, on the home page.

Exploration

Complete the following to the best of your knowledge:

1. Make a list of what you believe your viewers already know about the subject of your Website.
2. Make a list of what you perceive will be new information or terms to them.
3. Make a list of what you want them to glean from your Website. What would you like them to learn or do as a result of visiting your site?

Which are the simplest concepts (or what is most obvious and known)? Which are the most complex (or what is least obvious and probably unknown)?

Study how other Websites help their visitors maneuver through their sites using hyperlinks. How do visitors get back to the home page from anywhere within the site, for instance? How do various Web pages connect with one another? Where would you place buttons to get visitors from one part of the site to another? What would those buttons say?

It is best to have buttons with consistent text on all your Web pages. You don't want to use the word *Home* on part of your website to take viewers back to the home page and then use the words *Back to home page* on other parts.

Words are the foundation of any Website, and they need to be considered first. When you build a house, no matter how beautiful you want it to be, you must start with a solid foundation. This same principle applies to building a Website. Your words are your foundation. Make sure that foundation is solid by doing sound, painstaking, consistent content planning.

PLAN AND ORGANIZE CONTENT FOR A SLIDE PRESENTATION

Creating content for an on-screen presentation may seem a daunting task. What should you include and leave out? How can you best organize your information to reach and positively impact your viewers? How much is too much? How little is too little? Putting a presentation together well is even more important these days since they can be saved onto CD-ROMs and widely distributed. PowerPoints aren't just for the big screen anymore! I will be primarily referencing Microsoft PowerPoint, since it is the most widely used slide presentation software. But what I suggest here can also be applied to Apple's Keynote and other software programs used for slide-style presentations.

The best way to create a slide presentation is to write one slide at a time without adding any effects, colors, or other design elements. Here are five ways to go:

1. **Use presentation software.** Begin a new presentation, start with a title slide, and then write each slide using black text on a white background. Resize the text if you wish, but at this point don't add any elements to the slide presentation except words. Don't even begin to ponder colors, images, backgrounds, and special effects until you have a solid script. View your slide show to see how your words are flowing. Have someone else view it and give you feedback. Seeing your script in simple black and white can really show you how well the writing works. You can't dress up poor writing with special effects. All that does is draw more attention to bad writing.

So start with the writing. Later you can use phrases, bullets, and other techniques outlined in other chapters of this book to ensure that you aren't putting too many words on any one slide. Try to keep the number of slides between 20 and 35. More than 35 slides requires an intermission!

Once you have written your script, you can print it out in Handouts view so you have four to six slides printed per page. That will allow you to take and read your script, or have someone else read it. You can scribble any changes on the paper and incorporate them into the slides later. You will notice spelling and grammatical errors that may have eluded you if they were hidden by fancy fonts and effects.

Remember that you are never finished when you write the first draft of your script. Leave it alone for a while, and then come back to it. You will inevitably think of things you want to add or subtract from the text.

Your first slide should be your title slide (and your copyright), and your last slide should be your resources slide (if applicable).

2. **Use 4 × 6 inch note cards.** Write your content on 4 × 6 inch index cards. Let each card represent one slide.

3. **Use typing paper.** Turn it sideways to simulate a slide.

4. **Make a storyboard.** I admit that I don't often use storyboarding because I can't draw. Even my stick figures need artistic help. But if you can draw at all, try the two-column storyboard. One column displays descriptions or drawings of the visuals, and the other contains the written script. Called call-outs, the description columns don't list every exact visual, but they suggest the type of visuals, photos, or graphics.

5. **Create a logic tree.** Another good organizational tool is called a logic tree. You draw squares and write in your main point, then branch out by creating sub-boxes and their supporting boxes. It's similar to creating a linear outline, except that the structure is branching. (There's a good link on the CD-ROM to a logic tree example.)

We will be expanding upon what we have covered here in subsequent chapters. But this chapter helps you create solid foundations for high-quality Websites and multimedia presentations.

Review

1. If you use anyone's text verbatim, you must give the author credit and quote the material properly. Even though the material exists in cyberspace, copyright rules apply.

2. Put textual material in quotes. If it is a short quote, you can use it without seeking permission of the author. If you are basing an entire slide presentation or Web page on someone else's work, however, it is wise to try and get written permission from the author or owner of the material.

3. At a minimum, you must cite the title of the Website, the section you used, and the Website address that includes that section.

4. When linking to someone else's Website, be sure that your link makes it clear to visitors that they are no longer on your Website.

5. You must clearly acknowledge the source of any image you put on your Website or into your slide presentation unless it is copyright-free clip art.

6. You cannot copy and paste text from a Website or download an image without acknowledging the source in some formal fashion.

7. For slide presentations, it is best to have a final "Resources" slide that spells out the source of any quotes or images used within your presentation.

8. For a Website, credit the information you have used somewhere on the Web page where it is found.

9. Keep up to date on multimedia copyright rules.

10. There are "fair use" provisions that allow you to use another's material for personal, educational, and noncommercial reasons. These provide a bit more flexibility than if you are using someone else's images or text to make money for yourself.

11. Just because your document appears on a computer screen rather than on paper does not make it any less legitimate in the eyes of the law. You can copyright the content and images on your Website or in your slide presentation.

12. Never forget that plagiarism is a crime, punishable in the United States by potentially huge fines. Plagiarism involves stealing the words and images conceived by another human being.

13. Think of your Website as an electronic book. The home page contains the table of contents, or navigation bar in Web lingo. Your navigation bar tells viewers what all your Web pages contain.

14. Each Web page is a chapter in your electronic book. But unlike a traditional book, people will not read your pages in order. They may read the last page first. So all your pages need to connect with one another as well as stand alone. And all of them should lead viewers back to your home page. This can be accomplished by making sure there is a "Home" button on every page.

15. The home page is the first page to plan. The current trend is to have a home page that requires no scrolling.

16. Unlike a book, which is permanent once it has been committed to ink, your Web pages can be easily edited as the process of Web building continues.

17. Preparing content first helps designers envision what you want to say and how best to present it visually. If you are your own designer, the same principle holds true.

18. A rule of thumb is that the closer you are to the home page, the fewer words you should use. As you go deeper into the Website, you can create pages with more words.

19. Build new, complex information on the foundation of the simplest information. This provides needed background and a mental "staging area" for your viewers, as you introduce them to more complex ideas and data. People learn by building upon existing knowledge.

20. Words are the foundation of any Website. They need to be considered first.

21. The best way to create a slide presentation is to write one slide at a time without adding any effects, colors, or other design elements. Begin a new presentation, start with a title slide, and then write each slide using black text on a white background. Resize the text if

you wish, but don't add any elements to the first draft of the slide presentation except words.

22. Seeing your script in simple black and white can really show you how well the writing works. You can't dress up poor writing with special effects. All that does is draw more attention to bad writing.

Key Terms and Concepts

Address The uniform resource locator (URL) for a Website, such as www.specialspecies.com.

Copyright The legal protection afforded an intellectual property, such as original text and images.

Domain name The part of the Web address that usually reflects the title of a Website.

Fair use Legal provisions that allow you to use another's material for personal, educational, and noncommercial reasons.

Home page The first page of a Website.

Plagiarism The illegal act of stealing the words and/or images conceived by another human being and claiming them as one's own.

Web page Any single page of a Website.

Website The entire collection of Web pages and the home page.

Chapter Questions

1. What are the Four Essentials for a home page?
2. How many slides are recommended for a slide presentation?

Now You Try

On the CD-ROM, visit the recommended Helpful Websites for chapter 4 to find:

- A very user-friendly primer to legal issues surrounding copyrights
- The U.S. Copyright Office online
- Stanford University Libraries' guide to Copyright & Fair Use
- Columbia University Press's Guide to Online Style
- A compilation of citation styles
- A service for educators that helps them track down plagiarized student papers

- A clear and useful Web Site Planning and Design tutorial from Ball State University
- An easy-to-use guide for organizing a presentation using a logic tree

Write 15 interesting facts you learned from visiting these Websites. Identify where each fact came from (by Website title and Web page address).

Endnotes

1. *The Columbia world of quotations.* (1996). New York: Columbia University Press.
2. Rout, Lawrence. (2003, October 20). Editor's note. *The Wall Street Journal*, R2.
3. *The American Heritage dictionary of the English language* (4th ed.). (2000). Boston: Houghton Mifflin.
4. *Webster's revised unabridged dictionary.* (1998). Plainfield NJ: MICRA.
5. Library of Congress, Copyright Office. (2004, January). *In answer to your query: Fair use* (LOC Publication No. FL–102). Washington, DC: U.S. Government Printing Office. Available online at www.loc.gov/copyright/fls/fl102.pdf.
6. Ibid.
7. Ibid.
8. Ibid.

Answers for Chapter 4

Chapter Questions

1. **What are the Four Essentials for a home page?**

1. title
2. table of contents (navigation bar)
3. blurb
4. Introduction or (lead-in)

2. **How many slides are recommended for a slide presentation?**

Between 20 and 35 (the closer to 20, the better). More than 35 slides requires an intermission!

Make Your Words Work

We don't just borrow words; on occasion, English has pursued other languages down alleyways to beat them unconscious and rifle their pockets for new vocabulary.

—James D. Nicoll[1]

OBJECTIVES

This chapter will help you learn:

- The importance of proper spelling, grammar, and punctuation
- How to deal with slang, jargon, acronyms, and abbreviations
- What to consider when writing for an international audience

THE IMPORTANCE OF PROPER SPELLING, GRAMMAR, AND PUNCTUATION

First impressions count.

Multimedia has made communicating faster. In the "old" days, we had to type, print out, and mail written communications to one another. Now we can simply open an e-mail program, type a quick message, and hit "Send."

But exchanging speed for literacy is not an improvement. Glaring grammatical errors in e-mails and spelling mistakes in multimedia presentations are not acceptable (especially since most software programs now offer some kind of spell check function). The good news is that usually a mistake can be quickly and easily corrected, unlike with print publications, which may cost thousands of dollars to produce and cannot be easily corrected once they are published.

Credibility is based on many factors, not the least of which is what we say and how we say it. If we purport to put forth a professional, believable, and intelligent point of view, the presentation must be polished.

I recall watching a cable news network with ticker tape–style news summaries running nonstop while the anchorpeople delivered other stories. While an anchor was intoning an especially somber story related to the terrorist events of September 11 in New York, different ticker tape words about different stories were crawling below.

"New York's food panties nearly empty this year," read the words going by on the screen. The message rolled by repeatedly for over 15 minutes before someone in the cable newsroom fixed it to read, "New York's food pantries nearly empty this year." But that one-letter mistake created howls of laughter among TV audience members with whom I was sitting. It distracted viewers from the message, diminished the credibility of the news anchor (who was probably unaware of the error), and made the news look, well, silly.

Improper grammar, spelling, or punctuation can be completely distracting. Viewers will focus on it above all else. Consider, for example, an MSNBC ticker tape that reported on the "Salk Lake City" Olympics in 2002.

Recently I sat in front of my television for two hours and randomly switched channels among cable news networks. Here's what I saw flash by on their ticker tape news feeds:

Pron instead of *Porn* (MSNBC)

Payed instead of *Paid* (CNN)

Fox News had no errors. Apparently, the folks there know how to use Spell Check (or maybe even a dictionary!). When I'm writing, I use a dictionary or a Website such as www.dictionary.com.

When I'm teaching multimedia writing to kids, one of my favorite assignments is to ask them to watch TV news and write down all the misspelled words or grammatical errors they see in one hour. Seldom do the kids come back with nothing to report.

Another exercise I like to give kids is a page-long report with one misspelled word. They may or may not spot it. Then I include the same misspelled word as part of a two-column PowerPoint slide. Almost instantly, they find the word. The point is that a mistake may be somewhat noticeable in print but jump out when projected onto a screen.

Many times, I have been witness to a hardworking person giving a PowerPoint presentation that probably took weeks or more to prepare. Yet without fail, if there is one word misspelled on one PowerPoint slide, the audience begins to whisper, or chortle, or just stare as if trying to decide how the word should have been spelled. Whatever message was intended on that slide is lost.

Likewise, I have seen major grammatical or spelling errors on the home pages of business Websites. To me this says, "We don't quite have our act together." That's not a message of confidence I'd recommend sending to potential customers who have to decide whether or not to trust your online information and services.

So even though it may seem out of place to review grammar, punctuation, and spelling basics in a multimedia writing book, having a comfortable grasp of this chapter will ensure that your writing has grace and polish and projects a professional public image.

Exploration

Let's review the basic parts of speech. See if you can match these terms with their definitions. Put the number of the correct term in front of the corresponding definition; then visit the Key Terms and Concepts section at the end of this chapter for the answers.

1. Adjectives   5. Pronouns

2. Articles   6. Verbs

3. Adverbs   7. Conjunctions

4. Nouns   8. Prepositions

_____ Name persons, places, and things (man, Paris, happiness)

_____ Substitute for nouns (it, she, they)

_____ Are action words (run, jump, enjoy)

_____ Describe nouns and pronouns (beautiful, these, many)

_____ Are the three adjectives used to describe "which one" (a, an, the)

_____ Mainly describe verbs and adverbs (always, happily, too)

_____ Join words or groups of words (and, so, until)

_____ Relate position to a noun or pronoun (inside, near, around)

With today's ability to easily do spell checking and grammar checking, there is really little excuse for either kind of error. And there are professional editors available who will copyedit any content on a contractual basis if there is no editor on staff.

Additionally, there are many style guides on the market, as well as dictionaries. And resources continue to blossom online. There are online editing services, dictionaries, translators, and other services available.

Many community colleges offer basic classes to help you brush up on spelling, grammar, and writing skills. These courses are typically offered through English, business, and journalism departments. There are workbooks you can buy to practice your skills. There are also courses you can take online so that you can work at your own pace and convenience.

Remember that even the best grammar/spell check program can't be counted on to detect an incorrect choice of words (such as *panties* vs. *pantries* or *bear* vs. *bare*). Nor can it detect inflection or intention based on punctuation. Years ago, I saw in *Reader's Digest* an anecdote about a teacher who gave a class this sentence to correctly punctuate:

Woman without her man is lost

Many of the males in the class simply put a period at the end of the sentence so that it read:

Woman without her man is lost.

Interestingly, many of the females in the class chose to punctuate it this way:

Woman, without her, man is lost.

The sentence stayed the same, but the addition of commas completely changed its meaning! To this day, I use this sentence in all my business communications classes, often with the same result.

Just a few commas, or a missing letter, can alter your intended meaning entirely. Plus, it is important that you really know the meaning of the words you choose to use. I'm reminded of the time I took my young son to a friend's house and when he walked in, my son looked around and said, "Your house is really homely." My friend was somewhat taken aback, since the most common understanding of the word *homely* is plain and ugly. I asked my son what he meant, and he said, "You know, it's really comfortable and friendly in here." I said, "Do you mean that it's really homey?" "Yeah," he said, "that's what I meant—homey."

The common definition of *homey* is warm and homelike, although to some a *homey* is slang for someone who lives nearby. And when I looked up *homely* in the dictionary, it did say that *homely* could also be used to describe a homelike atmosphere, although that tends not to be a common usage. So you can see that evaluating and using just the right word is important.

You must be the ultimate overseer of whatever words, grammar, and punctuation you present in a multimedia environment. Otherwise, you may confuse, distract, or even insult a viewer without realizing it.

Most people have a pretty good sense of their own ability when it comes to spelling and grammar. If you are one of those people for whom spelling does not come easily, then make friends with a dictionary (even if it's an online dictionary such as www.dictionary.com). Like any other skill, the key is practice. Having trouble in these areas doesn't mean you aren't smart. It means you haven't practiced enough.

Whether or not you consider yourself adept at language skills, never edit yourself. Before anything you write faces public scrutiny, have someone else go over it word for word. Very often, we look at our own writing so many times, we fail to see obvious mistakes in spelling, grammar, punctuation, or sentence structure. Whether it's a paid professional or someone whose skills you trust, an editor is invaluable when it comes to polishing your writing.

Exploration

Read the following, and see how many mistakes you can find in spelling, grammar, or punctuation. Turn to page 94 for 55 answers.

In the last 20 years as concerns about the enviroment have increased more and more people have began planting gardens of native plants. A Native Plant is a plant that is indiginous to the region in witch it is planted. It hasnt been introduced from any other part of the world, either as a weed seed bought in on the shoes' of early settlers, nor as a purposely planted speciman. In early times, when settlers came from other countrys, they would offen bring seeds of grasses and other plants from they're Homelands. They new these kind of plants could be used as food for live stock or people. Setters also brought the seeds as a reminder of there "old country".

The problem being that many of these plants dis-placed the native plants that had evolved to serve the wild life of the region as food, or shelter. Sum of the native plants was used by the native americans as medicines. Lotsa other plants were chopped or mowed down to make weigh for farmers fields.

In later years, access pestisides and human encrochement elimenated evermore native plants. When the problem of extincion became knowen, Native Plant Groups were founded to try, and save, and restore, the natives.

People who now garden using native plants due so: to re-store history, to help native birds butterflies and other wildlife and to enjoy their intrensic beauty. Native plants are aclimated to local whether conditions and resistent to local pests, which means they usally do not knead special watering or pesticides to survive.

Native plant gardens are now very poplar threw out the united states and other parts of the word.

The following self-test will help you evaluate whether or not you need to review areas of spelling, grammar, and punctuation. After completing the exercises, turn to page 96 for the answers. If you miss more than three in any one section, you need to review that particular area of grammar, spelling, or punctuation.

No peeking! Good luck, and try to have fun with it.

Self-Test Questions

Please get out a piece of paper and number according to part 1, part 2, part 3, etc. Then answer the questions to the best of your ability.

Part 1 / Recognizing Incomplete Sentences

In traditional business writing, fragments (or incomplete sentences) are generally considered inappropriate. While it is true that the use of phrases rather than complete sentences is more accepted in multimedia, you should still be doing it on purpose and not by accident.

Read the following 10 sentences. If you think an item is a complete sentence (an independent clause with both a subject and a verb), mark it C (for complete). If you think the item is incomplete (a dependent clause lacking a subject or verb), mark it I (for incomplete).

1. Enjoying our trip to Europe
2. Soon we will be leaving
3. The scenery was fantastic
4. Getting very homesick though
5. We can't wait to get home
6. Lots of great memories to share
7. We hope you like this postcard
8. Meet us at the airport
9. Too tired to write more
10. We'll see you soon

Part 2 / Subject/Verb Agreement

Few things show a lack of sophistication more than using a plural verb form with a singular subject, or a singular verb form with a plural subject. For example, "Cissy were at the dance with her friend" is incorrect. Because Cissy is one person, she *was* at the dance with her friend.

Read the following 10 sentences. If you think the subject-verb agreement in a sentence is correct, mark your answer C (for correct). If you think a sentence is wrong, please rewrite it correctly.

1. John and I was first in line.
2. Where is my pants?
3. Those two brothers has them.
4. A group of teachers are in the hall.
5. The jury are coming back with a verdict.
6. Leland, Smith & Davis, Esq. are handling the lawsuit.
7. My boss, along with Mary and Bill, are going.
8. All the kids play outside on sunny days.
9. The contractor and his crew start tomorrow.
10. She is afraid of the dark.

Part 3 / Spelling

A major distraction in any presentation is a misspelled word. It attracts the eye and captures unwanted attention. Thanks to spell check programs, we don't need to be brilliant spellers all the time, but we should have a good working knowledge of the principles of spelling (and how to use a dictionary).

Be careful not to rely too heavily on spell check programs. Interestingly, I ran a spell check on the words below, and the program missed two words that I had purposely misspelled!

Decide if the following 20 words are spelled correctly. If you think a word is correct, mark your answer C (for correct). If you think it is incorrect, rewrite it correctly. Feel free to use a dictionary, especially if you don't know what a word means. All these words are commonly used in business, education, and journalism.

1. accommodate	11. lucrative
2. analyze	12. manuever
3. correspondance	13. momento
4. dissatasfied	14. misellaneous
5. extrordinary	15. necessitate
6. fascinating	16. occurance
7. gaurantee	17. participent
8. government	18. prefered
9. itinnerary	19. questionaire
10. jeapordize	20. summarized

Part 4 / Correct Word Choice

There can be a big difference between words that sound or look alike. In one of my evening business English classes, for example, I taught a college student who worked during the day as a receptionist. The problem for her at work was that she continuously wrote the word *massage* when she meant *message*. Her supervisor was not amused. Choosing the right word matters.

Read the 15 sentences below, and pick the correct words from each selection. If in doubt, use the dictionary.

1. She was an (imminent/eminent) attorney who (passed/past) the bar exam easily.
2. She gave me good legal (advice/advise) and (counsel/council).
3. (Every one/Everyone) of you is expected to visit the new job (site/cite/sight).
4. Be careful not to (lose/loose) (your/you're) book.
5. (They're/There/Their) going to move soon.
6. I (hear/here) that (its/it's) a difficult golf (coarse/course).
7. The (personal/personnel) department does all the hiring.
8. Our school (principal/principle) really stands on (principal/principle).
9. I can't (except/accept) the fact that Jane has that (affect/effect) on me.

10. At the end of our company's (fiscal/physical) year, we (threw/through) a party.

11. We'll need some (Capitol/capital) if we're going to visit the U.S. (Capitol/capital).

12. (Whose/Who's) coming to watch the old building get (razed/raised)?

13. We have (access/excess) (stationary/stationery) in the supply room.

14. We need to (elicit/illicit) donations before we can (precede/proceed).

15. She doesn't have any other (choice/chose/choose) that makes (cents/sense/scents).

Part 5 / Correct Tense

Matching the verb form to the correct time frame—past, present, or future—is important if your content is to appear polished and professional.

Read the following 10 sentences. They are all incorrect. Rewrite each sentence using the appropriate verb forms. Consider, for example, the following sentence:

Tomorrow, Selma be off on her trip.

This can be rewritten to read:

Tomorrow, Selma will be off on her trip.

Or even:

Tomorrow, Selma will be going on her trip.

Sometimes, there is more than one correct way to use verb forms.

1. He has already began the speech.

2. We been there before.

3. They hanged up all the coats.

4. I seen it with my own eyes.

5. Anna has went there before.

6. Steve drunk all the milk.

7. The book was hid on the shelf.

8. How you doing?

9. We should of gone yesterday.

10. He done decided to go.

Part 6 / Adjectives and Adverbs

An essential part of writing good multimedia content is descriptive writing. Using adjectives and adverbs correctly can add important dimension to your text.

Read the following 20 sentences. Pay close attention to any adverbs (which generally describe verbs) and adjectives (which generally describe nouns). If you think the use of adjectives and/or adverbs is correct, mark your answer C (for correct). If you think there is an error, write the correct form of the adjective or adverb on your paper. Take this sentence for example: *She types quick.* The correct adverb is *quickly.* You would write the word *quickly* as your answer. (Hint: Only three of the following sentences are correct.)

1. Winston felt bad about his mistake.
2. He speaks real clear.
3. That cake tasted deliciously.
4. I did good on the test.
5. She is really smart.
6. This kinds of pens are my favorite.
7. Them boys are in big trouble.
8. These are my mother's eyeglasses.
9. That there bike is mine.
10. He's a FBI agent.
11. This types of problems always happen.
12. What a angry customer!
13. Azusa doesn't need no help.
14. Do you have a umbrella?
15. She couldn't never do that.
16. Lucy doesn't know nothing about it.
17. Jose plays the goodest guitar.
18. Green is the best of the two colors.
19. Of all Ruby's rosebushes, this one is prettier.
20. He's the nicest of the twins.

Part 7 / Pronouns

Pronouns substitute for nouns. Make sure that the pronoun substitute is accurate. This will add clarity and sophistication to your content.

Traditionally, male pronouns were used as generic singular pronouns. *It is time for everyone to turn in <u>his</u> paper.* This usage is not always considered appropriate anymore, in that it may suggest male chauvinism. Be aware of this possibility. You might want to substitute *his or her, his and her, his/her,* or even *s/he. It is time for everyone to turn in* **his/her** *paper.* Better yet, try to avoid the problem altogether:

Turn in your papers now. (Use the command imperative verb form.)

Everyone must turn in papers now. (Eliminate the troublesome pronoun.)

Students must turn in their papers now. (Replace singular with plural pronoun.)

Read the following 15 sentences, and choose the correct pronoun. Remember that plural pronouns need to match plural nouns or other pronouns.

1. Everyone needs to get (his or her/their) act together.
2. Each of the employees tried (his or her/their) best.
3. (Them/They) are already there.
4. (Us/We) workers want a raise.
5. Bill and (he/him) left work already.
6. Everyone is helping except Mary and (she/her).
7. Mami works faster than(her/she).
8. Bob sat with Irene and (I/me) on the train.
9. CJ and (I/me) will go first.
10. He did it (hisself/himself).
11. No one is sweeter than (her/she).
12. The company released (their/it's/its) earning statement.
13. The man (who/whom) I saw is Gary's uncle.
14. The jury reached (their/it's/its) verdict in two hours.
15. (Their/They're/There) coming over in an hour.

Part 8 / Plurals

Write the plural forms of these 10 words. Feel free to use a dictionary.

1. company
2. tax
3. boss
4. data
5. memo
6. curriculum
7. medium
8. crisis
9. research
10. foot

Part 9 / Punctuation

I may have saved the worst for last, but punctuation is vital to clear communication and conveyance of meaning. For example, how would you punctuate these two sentences?

Can you believe that he asked

The boys parents doctor and nurse discussed the case

Depending on the meaning you are trying to convey, you could punctuate the sentences in different ways. Consider:

"Can you believe that?" he asked.

Can you believe that he asked?

The boys, parents, doctor, and nurse discussed the case. (Everyone talked about the case.)

The boy's parents' doctor and nurse discussed the case. (The doctor and nurse of a boy's parents talked about the case.)

The boy's parent's doctor and nurse discussed the case. (The doctor and nurse of one of the boy's parents talked about the case.)

The boys' parent's doctor. . . (refers to more than one boy and only one parent's doctor).

The boys' parents' doctor. . . (refers to more than one boy and both parents' doctor).

Notice how only apostrophes and commas are used to completely change the context of what is basically the same sentence.

Never underestimate the importance of a properly (or improperly) placed punctuation mark (including, but not limited to, apostrophes, commas, parentheses, periods, exclamation points, question marks, colons, semicolons, hyphens, dashes, and quotes).

Apostrophes

Apostrophes are used to show ownership, to designate contractions, and to clarify plurals. See if you can properly place apostrophes in these five phrases.

1. the boys book
2. two months pay
3. the womans group
4. couldnt make it
5. Oakland As baseball team

Commas

Commas are hard to master. They are used to separate ideas or elements within a sentence, but the temptation is to use too many. Guess how many commas are needed in each sentence below.

1. Tonight Bob is cooking rice beans and cornbread.
2. On our trip we visited Rome and Paris and Madrid.
3. John I know you want to go to the movies but we don't have the money.
4. When we went to Florida we did a lot of swimming.
5. When you write write clearly.

Quotation Marks

Whenever you use someone else's exact words, you need to acknowledge that use in an official way. Shorter quoted sentences and paragraphs can be acknowledged using quotation marks. Quotation marks are also used to identify certain titles. Add quotes and punctuation marks to these five sentences.

1. To quote the late President Franklin Roosevelt we have nothing to fear but fear itself
2. There's a fire in the theater screamed the usher
3. Do you have any idea what I just said he asked
4. I'm afraid the coach said we're going to have to let you go
5. I Want To Hold Your Hand was an early Beatles' hit

Punctuation Potpourri

Now that you're a punctuation expert, here are 10 final sentences for you to judge. Review each one and decide if it is correct or not. If you think it is correct, mark your answer C (for correct). If you think any part of the punctuation is incorrect, mark your answer I (for incorrect). These sentences utilize punctuation we have covered so far, plus parentheses, colons, semicolons, hyphens, and dashes.

Feel free to use the dictionary to look up word combinations using hyphens. The dictionary is the best place to see if words are hyphenated (far-flung), combined as one word (baseball), or presented as two words (foul line).

Getting punctuation right is important if you want to convey the correct meaning. For example, *look out* (two separate words) means to watch where you're going, but a *lookout* (two words combined as one) is a high place or someone standing guard, watching for the enemy's approach. *Lock out* (two separate words) means to bar the door, but *lockout* (two words combined as one) is what a company does to employees sometimes during a labor dispute.

Finally, remember that there is a difference between a hyphen and a dash (two hyphens, which word-processing software will normally convert to one dash). A hyphen is used to separate parts in a word; a dash is used to separate parts in a sentence or phrase.

1. "That's fantastic!" he exclaimed.
2. I really need some up-to-date weather reports for sixty-two hard-to-find locations.
3. Benito Santiago—a veteran professional baseball player—is considered one of the game's best catchers.
4. Our dog always has one thing on his mind: food.
5. Jamal works hard at tennis; then he comes home to rest.

6. The directions (see page 16) are in English and Spanish.
7. "Do you have any idea how hard I workout?" she asked.
8. It's important to monitor children's activities on the Internet.
9. Jana and I have the same color hair.
10. Wow! You've finished all the exercises.

So how did you do? Hopefully you aced this whole section (*aced* is a slang expression, of course, for doing well or earning an A). And speaking of slang, let's move on.

DEALING WITH SLANG, JARGON, ACRONYMS, AND ABBREVIATIONS
Slang

Slang is commonly thought of as the language of the street or terms that reflect a particular culture or group. What works in one culture or group, however, may not translate to another. Or it may translate in a different, unexpected, and unwelcome way.

So if you choose to use slang terminology, remember that you are limiting your audience to whatever group will comprehend it. If you are doing this intentionally, that's fine, but if you aren't aware that you are doing it, you could be losing or offending a group you'd like to reach.

After I taught a group of junior high students how to create their own animated life stories, they told me it was "sick." Unbeknownst to me until that moment, *sick* is a good thing, just like *bad* used to mean good not that long ago. But for a moment there, I questioned my professional judgment before they saw my confusion and explained to me what they meant by *sick*.

Similarly, my teenage son and his friends are in the habit of inserting the word *all* and/or *like* into nearly every sentence. "I was *all* bummed out because the concert was *like* not that great and we were *all like* sitting in bad seats." (In this case, *bad* means bad, not good as in "It's all good"—another expression that includes *all* and *good*, which in this case really *does* mean good. And that's *like* perfectly clear, I'm sure.)

After a while, I realized I was counting how many *alls* I heard instead of listening to what was being said to me. I explained to my son that if he wanted me to focus on his message, he needed to drop at least the *alls* because they were too distracting. He tried to talk to me without using *all* in every sentence and admitted it was hard because he was so used to the slang of his particular group, he couldn't move out of it to reach a different (older) listener.

Similarly, if we as communicators are going to broaden our audience, particularly on a Website that is accessible worldwide, we really need to question if our language style is so slang-based that it's confusing or annoying.

Jargon

Jargon is known as terminology particular to a certain profession. Every profession has its own jargon. Sometimes we get so dazzled by our ability to speak and understand "inside the zone" jargon, we fail to move "outside the box" to create a "win-win" communication vehicle and "move forward" with our audience—the public. Maybe we think *IT* stands for Information Technology, but to the great wide world out there, *IT* might just be *it* in capital letters.

To assume everyone knows all the terminology with which we are intimately familiar is a big mistake. In journalism school, I learned these words: Never Assume. They are words worth remembering whenever you create content for an audience outside your immediate professional circle.

To find out if you are reaching all the intended viewers, show your content to a focus group comprised of people outside your frame of reference. By focus group, I do not necessarily mean an elaborate, research-based cross section of humanity. Ask your grandmother to read it. Run it by a variety of people from everyday life, and see what they think. If you aren't brave enough to do that, you probably don't have much faith in the content anyway. Don't discount what these people have to say. If they don't get it, if a term is unclear, or if they have no idea what a phrase means, they are doing you a huge favor by telling you. So thank them. Buy them lunch.

Acronyms

Acronyms can also prove tricky for both domestic and international viewers. I have spoken to many American combat veterans who would never buy the Korean-imported KIA automobile, because to them those letters stand for "Killed In Action."

Speaking of cars, in what has now become a legendary example in marketing and public relations lore, the Chevrolet Nova proved unpopular in Latin America because "no va" is Spanish for "it doesn't go."

Abbreviations

Abbreviations can complicate matters as well. In the past year, for example, writers of those ticker tape news headlines on cable news networks have taken to creating word abbreviations that are arbitrary, confusing, or downright nonsensical. One cable news network, for example, uses INTEL as an abbreviation for intelligence agency. But because INTEL is the name of a major corporation, it is confusing to read how INTEL is involved in tracking down terrorists. This same network uses CT as an abbreviation for the word *court*. So whenever they write about suspects appearing in CT, it looks as if criminal suspects everywhere are appearing in Connecticut! (It doesn't help that they write their text in ALL CAPITAL LETTERS.) This particular network also has a habit of just making up abbreviations. Recently they injected MI into the middle of a sentence, and I tried for many minutes to imagine what it stood for (which, of course, means I was tuned out as far as the rest of the content was concerned). To me, as an educator, MI stands for multiple intelligences. Then again, it could be Michigan.

Abbreviations are also acceptable in multimedia writing, although you must make sure any abbreviations you use are readily understood. The same abbreviations may have more than one meaning. In the United States, PRI stands for Public Radio International. But in Mexico, the PRI is a major political party, Partido Revolucionario Institucional. It also stands for the Paleontological Research Institution (in Ithaca, New York); the Performance Review Institute (of Warrendale, Philadelphia, and Yate, Bristol, England); the Partito Repubblicano Italiano (of Italy); the Pupil Researcher Initiative run by the Centre for Science Education at Sheffield Hallam University (in the United Kingdom); and—well, you get the idea. (To discover just how common your "common" abbreviation might be, type it into the search box of a search engine like Google.com. You might discover there are several different uses for the same abbreviations. Also check the dictionary.)

If you are using abbreviations, they should at least have some standard conventions attached to them. If you try to reduce all of multimedia writing to the level of instant messaging, you may save time and space but lose meaning.

WHAT TO CONSIDER WHEN WRITING FOR AN INTERNATIONAL AUDIENCE

Some 400 million people throughout the world speak English. That's a lot of people! But consider these statistics as well: Close to 1 billion speak some form of Chinese; 305 million speak Urdu; 265 million, Russian; 245 million, French; 119 million, German; 117 million, Japanese. There are thousands of additional languages and language dialects, each with its own special character. And just in case you've overlooked them, there are more than 140 languages spoken in the United States.

Words can have subtle, possibly unintended, connotations. Twenty years ago, someone who lived outside the United States was said to be a *foreigner*. Today that word has a somewhat negative connotation in the world of cyber-communications. A *foreigner* is an outsider, someone who may not be welcomed or understood. Now that the Internet has opened many countries and cultures to one another, and the objective is to reach out and communicate, consider these alternatives:

"He was born overseas," rather than "He is a foreigner."

"She is Asian," rather than "She is Oriental."

"The company is based in Singapore," rather than "It's in a foreign country."

Words such as *international* and *global* have a more positive connotation than *foreign*.

Don't assume that the way you speak or write is universal, even if it seems predominant in your circle of experience. Ask people in America how they feel, and they may likely answer "fine." Ask people in Asia how they feel, and they may likely answer, "with my fingers."

When your writing will be seen internationally:

- Use simple language and active voice.
- Choose short words over longer ones ("start" rather than "commence," for example).
- Avoid metaphors unique to your culture ("great success" rather than "grand slam" or "big hit").
- Make careful choices about font colors (many vivid colors have cultural implications).
- Be aware of gender issues (addressing girls and women varies depending on culture).
- Stay away from the cliché.

If viewers for whom English is a second language will see your presentation in English, you may wish to hire a "localizer" to review your content for clarity and cultural sensitivity. You may want to arrange a contract with a native-born English language instructor at a college overseas who can evaluate your content.

If you want to translate your multimedia endeavor into another language, you will need to make certain decisions:

- Take into account dialects. Countries may have more than one dialect. The two predominant dialects in China, for example, are what Westerners call Cantonese and Mandarin.

- Consider what should be translated. If you own or operate a company, should your company's name and products be translated? If you are a teacher, should theory titles such as Constructivism be translated? If you report news, how do you determine proper phrasing? As a journalism instructor once told me, "One man's rebel outlaw is another man's freedom fighter."

Exploration

Do you know where Urdu is spoken? If not, research it. For extra credit, find out how to say "hello," "good-bye," and "thank you" in the Urdu language.

How many Chinese dialects are there? What are they? Where are they spoken?

Name the official language of each of the following:

Mozambique

Tajikistan

Tokelau

Monaco

Suriname

Name 10 countries where English is considered a foreign language.

Review

1. What we say and how we say it affect our credibility.
2. Improper grammar, spelling, or punctuation can be completely distracting.
3. Even the best grammar/spell check program can't always detect an incorrect word choice.
4. You must be the ultimate overseer of the words, grammar, and punctuation you present.
5. The use of phrases rather than complete sentences is more accepted in multimedia writing than in traditional business writing.
6. Using adjectives and adverbs correctly can add important dimension to your text.
7. Never underestimate the importance of a properly (or improperly) placed punctuation mark.
8. Don't assume that the way you speak or write is universal.

Key Terms and Concepts

Acronym   A word formed from initials, such as KIA for Killed In Action.

Adjectives   Describe nouns and pronouns (*beautiful, these, many*).

Adverbs   Mainly describe verbs and adverbs (*always, happily, too*).

Articles   The three adjectives used to describe "which one" (*a, an, the*).

Conjunctions   Join words or groups of words (*and, so, until*).

Dash   Two hyphens (or the equivalent); used to separate words or phrases.

Fragment   An incomplete sentence (lacking a subject or verb).

Hyphen   Half a dash; used in many compound words and numbers.

Jargon   Terminology particular to a certain profession.

Nouns   Name persons, places, and things (*man, Paris, happiness*).

Prepositions   Relate position to a noun or pronoun (*inside, near, around*).

Pronouns   Substitute for nouns (*it, she, they*).

Slang   Words, phrases, or terms that reflect a particular culture or group.

Verbs   Action words (*run, jump, enjoy*).

Chapter Questions

1. What is the purpose of a comma?
2. What is the purpose of an apostrophe?

Now You Try

On the CD-ROM, visit the recommended Helpful Websites for chapter 5 to find:

- An online dictionary Website that includes translation dictionaries, style guides, a thesaurus, and word games (some services cost money)
- A Website devoted to the languages of the world
- An article on what to consider when writing for an international audience
- A chance to assess if you understand global Web design and the dimensions of culture

Write 15 interesting facts you learned from visiting these Websites. Identify where each fact came from (by Website title and Web page address).

Endnote

1. *The Columbia world of quotations.* (1996). New York: Columbia University Press.

Answers for Chapter 5

Exploration

The following paragraphs contain corrections (in boldface) to the exercise on page 80.

> In the last 20 years as concerns about the **environment** have **increased, more** and more people **have begun** planting gardens of native plants. A **native plant** is a plant that is **indigenous** to the region in **which** it is planted. It **hasn't** been introduced from any other part of the world, either as a weed seed **brought** in on the **shoes** of early settlers, **or** as a purposely planted **specimen**. In early **times when** settlers came from other **countries,** they would **often** bring seeds of grasses and other plants from **their homelands**. They **knew** these **kinds** of plants could be used as food for **livestock** or people. **Settlers** also brought the seeds as a reminder of **their** "old country."
>
> The problem **is** that many of these plants **displaced** the native plants that had evolved to serve the **wildlife** of the region as **food or** shelter. **Some** of the native plants **were** used by the **Native Americans** as medicines. **Lots of** other plants were chopped or mowed down to make **way** for farmer**s'** fields.
>
> In later years, **excess pesticides** and human **encroachment eliminated ever more** native plants. When the problem of **extinction** became **known, native plant groups** were founded **to try and save and restore** the natives.
>
> People who now garden using native plants **do so to restore** history, to help **native birds, butterflies, and other wildlife,** and to enjoy their **intrinsic** beauty. Native plants are **acclimated** to local **weather** conditions and **resistant** to local pests, which means they **usually** do not **need** special watering or pesticides to survive.
>
> Native plant gardens are now very **popular throughout** the **United States** and other parts of the **world.**

Let's review the corrections:

1. The correct spelling is **environment.**
2. **increased, more:** A comma is necessary after an introductory series of words that includes any form of a verb.
3. Use **have begun,** not *have began.*
4. The term **native plant** does not require capitalization because it is a descriptive phrase, not a title or official name.
5. The correct spelling is **indigenous.**

6. The correct word is **which,** not *witch.*

7. An apostrophe is needed in **hasn't** to indicate the absence of the letter *o* (as in *has not*).

8. The word **brought** means *to bring.* The word *bought* means *to purchase.*

9. An apostrophe is not necessary here because the word **shoes** is plural but not possessive.

10. Use **or** with either, and *nor* with *neither.*

11. The correct spelling is **specimen.**

12. **times when:** No comma is required.

13. **Countries,** the plural of *country,* is misspelled.

14. The correct spelling is **often.**

15. The correct word is **their,** not *they're* (which is a contraction for *they are*).

16. The word **homelands** does not require capitalization because it is a term, not a title or official name.

17. The correct word is **knew** (the past tense of *know*), not *new* (the opposite of old).

18. Use these **kinds** (plural combination) or *this kind* (singular combination).

19. **Livestock** is a compound noun written as one word.

20. The correct spelling is **settlers.**

21. The correct word is **their,** not *there* (which identifies a location).

22. **country."** In most cases, the punctuation goes inside quotation marks.

23. Use **is** rather than *being* (which turns the sentence into an incomplete fragment).

24. **Displaced** does not require a hyphen.

25. **Wildlife** is a compound noun referring to non-domesticated animals. On the other hand, *wild life* describes a rowdy lifestyle.

26. **food or:** No comma is needed.

27. The correct word is **some,** not *sum.*

28. Use **were** rather than *was* because the subject *(some)* is plural.

29. **Native Americans** should be capitalized because it is the name of a recognized race of people.

30. Use **lots of** because there is no such word as *lotsa.*

31. The correct word is **way,** not *weigh.*

32. **Farmers'** requires an apostrophe because it is possessive (the farmers own the fields).

33. The correct word is **excess** (too much), not *access* (a means of entry).

34. The correct spelling is **pesticides.**

35. The correct spelling is **encroachment.**

36. The correct spelling is **eliminated.**

37. **Ever more** are two separate words.

38. The correct spelling is **extinction.**

39. The correct spelling is **known.**

40. **Native plant groups** does not require capitalization because it is a descriptive phrase, not a title or official name.

41. **to try and save and restore:** If the conjunction *and* precedes each item in a series, leave out commas.

42. The correct word is **do,** not *due.*

43. No colon is needed after the word *so* because it does not follow a full independent clause.

44. **Restore** does not require a hyphen.

45. **native birds, butterflies, and other wildlife:** Insert commas within a series of three or more items or phrases.

46. The correct spelling is **intrinsic.**

47. The correct spelling is **acclimated.**

48. The correct word is **weather,** not *whether.*

49. The correct spelling is **resistant.**

50. The correct spelling is **usually.**

51. The correct word is **need,** not *knead.*

52. The correct spelling is **popular,** not *poplar.*

53. The correct word is **throughout,** not *threw out.*

54. **United States** should be capitalized because it is the name of a country.

55. The correct word is **world,** not *word.*

Self-Test Questions

Below are the answers to exercises on pages 80–88.

Part 1 / Recognizing Incomplete Sentences

1. I		6. I	
2. C		7. C	
3. C		8. C	
4. I		9. I	
5. C		10. C	

Let's review the corrections:

Just because a sentence is short does not mean it isn't complete. In multimedia writing, short sentences are often preferred. Also, the subject can be understood without actually being seen.

For example, in number 7 the sentence would be written *Hope you like this postcard*, and the subject would be understood to be *I*. *I hope you like this postcard*. Even without the subject appearing in the sentence, the sentence is complete.

Finally, a complete sentence must have a legitimate verb that tells what the subject does, has, or is. Sometimes the verb (especially one ending with the letters *ing*) requires a "helper" verb, such as *is, are, was, were, will, can, could, would, might,* or *may*. Verb forms using the word *to* (e.g., *to write*) are not actually serving as verbs.

Part 2 / Subject/Verb Agreement

1. John and **I were** first in line.
2. Where **are** my pants?
3. Those two brothers **have** them.
4. A group of teachers **is** in the hall.
5. The jury **is** coming back with a verdict.
6. Leland, Smith & Davis, Esq. **is** handling the lawsuit.
7. My boss, along with Mary and Bill, **is** going.
8. C
9. C
10. C

Let's review the corrections:

1. *John and I* is a plural combination subject. Use **were** (plural), not *was* (singular).
2. Words such as *pants* and *scissors* are considered plural subjects (pants have two legs). Use **are** (plural), not *is* (singular).
3. *Brothers* is plural. Use **have** (plural), not *has* (singular).
4. *Group* is considered one unit. Use **is** (singular), not *are* (plural).
5. *Jury* is considered one unit. Use **is** (singular), not *are* (plural).
6. *Leland, Smith & Davis, Esq.* is *one* law firm. Use **is** (singular), not *are* (plural).
7. *Boss* is the subject (*Mary and Bill* are not included in the subject because they are introduced by the phrase *along with*). Use **is** (singular), not *are* (plural).

Numbers 8–10 are correct.

Often when a verb is used with a singular subject, you add an *s* or an *s* construction at the end of the verb. Dogs run. The dog runs. Birds fly. The bird flies. Consider if sentence 9 read: "The contractor starts tomorrow." It would be correct to add an *s* after the verb *start*. But because the sentence involves the contractor and his crew (plural), there is no *s* after the verb *start*.

Part 3 / Spellling

1. C
2. C
3. correspondence
4. dissatisfied
5. extraordinary
6. C
7. guarantee
8. C
9. itinerary
10. jeopardize
11. C
12. maneuver
13. memento
14. miscellaneous
15. C
16. occurrence
17. participant
18. preferred
19. questionnaire
20. C

Part 4 / Correct Word Choice

1. She was an **eminent** attorney who **passed** the bar exam easily.
2. She gave me good legal **advice** and **counsel**.
3. **Every one** of you is expected to visit the new job **site**.
4. Be careful not to **lose your** book.
5. **They're** going to move soon.
6. I **hear** that **it's** a difficult golf **course**.
7. The **personnel** department does all the hiring.
8. Our school **principal** really stands on **principle**.

9. I can't **accept** the fact that Jane has that **effect** on me.

10. At the end of our company's **fiscal** year, we **threw** a party.

11. We'll need some **capital** if we're going to visit the U.S. **Capitol**.

12. **Who's** coming to watch the old building get **razed**?

13. We have **excess stationery** in the supply room.

14. We need to **elicit** donations before we can **proceed**.

15. She doesn't have any other **choice** that makes **sense**.

Part 5 / Correct Tense

1. He **has** already **begun** the speech.

2. We **have been** there before.

3. They **hung** up all the coats.

4. I **saw** it with my own eyes.

5. Anna **has gone** there before.

6. Steve **drank** all the milk.

7. The book **was hidden** on the shelf.

8. How **are** you **doing?**

9. We **should have gone** yesterday.

10. He **has decided** to go.

Part 6 / Adjectives and Adverbs

1. C

2. He speaks **really clearly**.

3. That cake tasted **delicious**.

4. I did **well** on the test.

5. C

6. **These** kinds of pens are my favorite.

7. **Those** boys are in big trouble.

8. C

9. **That** bike is mine.

10. He's **an** FBI agent.

11. **These** types of problems always happen.

12. What **an** angry customer!

13. Azusa doesn't need **any** help.

14. Do you have **an** umbrella?

15. She **couldn't ever** do that. Or: She **could never** do that.

16. Lucy **doesn't know anything** about it. Or: Lucy **knows nothing** about it.

17. Jose plays the **best** guitar. Or: Jose plays guitar **best**.
18. Green is the **better** of the two colors.
19. Of all Ruby's rosebushes, this one is **prettiest**.
20. He's the **nicer** of the twins.

Let's review the corrections:

1–2. Words that describe verbs are called adverbs. To create adverbs, you often add the letters *ly*. **Really clearly** describes how he speaks (verb).

3. The word **delicious** describes the cake, not the action of tasting, so it is an adjective (not an adverb needing an *ly* at the end).

4. *Good* is an adjective. **Well** is an adverb correctly describing how I *did* (verb).

6–7, 11. *These* and *those* are plural. When used to describe, they must correspond with the plural noun. *That* and *this* are singular, so they accompany singular nouns. Use **these kinds** or **this kind; this type, these types, or those types; those boys, this boy,** or **that boy.**

9. Word combinations such as *this here, that there, them there, these here,* and *done did* are not standard English.

10, 12, 14. Generally, you use *a* before any word beginning with a consonant (a dog, a cat, a tree) and *an* before any word beginning with a vowel (an umbrella, an onion, an auto). But there are important exceptions (a union representative, an FBI agent). The exceptions mostly occur because of the way the beginning of the word *sounds*. For example, the beginning of the word *honest* sounds like *o* rather than *h*, so *an honest person* would be correct. Because of pronunciation, when the following consonants stand alone or begin an abbreviation (such as FBI), they use *an* rather than *a*: F (He got *an* F), H, L, M, N, R, S, X.

13, 15–16. **Doesn't** need **no** constitutes what is called a double negative. It is a no-no (no pun intended). Don't combine two negative words, such as I *don't* want *none*; he *shouldn't never* have said that; I *couldn't* get *no* date; *nobody won't* go.

17–20. As a general rule, when comparing two items (two colors, twins, etc.), an adjective ends with the letters *er* (nicer, prettier). When comparing three or more items, an adjective ends with the letters *est* (nicest, prettiest). Do not use *gooder* or *goodest*. Use *good, better,* and *best* (note that *better*, which ends in *er*, compares two things, and that *best*, which ends in *est*, compares three or more).

Part 7 / Pronouns

1. Everyone needs to get **his or her** act together.
2. Each of the employees tried **his or her** best.
3. **They** are already there.
4. **We** workers want a raise.
5. Bill and **he** left work already.
6. Everyone is helping except Mary and **her**.
7. Mami works faster than **she**.
8. Bob sat with Irene and **me** on the train.
9. CJ and **I** will go first.
10. He did it **himself**.
11. No one is sweeter than **she**.
12. The company released **its** earning statement.
13. The man **whom** I saw is Gary's uncle.
14. The jury reached **its** verdict in two hours.
15. **They're** coming over in an hour.

Let's review the corrections:

1–2. **Everyone** and **each** are singular pronouns (referring to every *one* individual and each *one*). Use *his*, *her*, or *his or her*. It is also acceptable to type *his/her*.

3. Never use *them* before a verb (are, will be, have, can, etc.). Use **they.**

4. Try omitting the noun (in this case, *workers*), and see if *us* or *we* sounds better in its place. *Us want a raise* sounds funny. *We want a raise* sounds correct. So use **we**. Consider another example: *Please give us teachers your attention*. Omit the word *teachers* (the noun), and it reads *Please give us your attention*. This sounds better than *Please give we your attention*, so in this case, you would use *us*.

5. Say the sentence aloud starting with the pronoun. Which sounds better: *Him left work already* or *he left work already*. The correct answer is **he**.

6, 8–9. These sentences are tricky because they contain compound word groups. The rule of thumb is to mentally omit the words that accompany the pronoun, such as "Mary and" (in number 6) or "Irene and" (in number 8). Once these extra words are gone, the correct pronoun is the one that can function alone in the sentence: "Everyone is helping except **her**." and "**I** will go first."

7, 11. Insert the word *does* or *is* at the end of each sentence. Mami works faster than *she does, she is, her is, her does*. Notice that the sentence makes sense if you end it with *she does*. So use **she**. No one is sweeter than *she does, she is, her is, her does*. Notice that the sentence makes sense if it ends with *she is*. So use **she**.

10. The words *hisself, theirself, theirselves,* and *mineself* are not standard English and should be avoided unless used on purpose for effect. Use *himself, herself, themselves, mine,* or *myself*.

12, 14. *Company* and *jury* are single entities, so they are treated as single nouns. This is also true for the name of a firm or company (Smith, Jones & Young, Inc.) even if it includes more than one proper name: *Procter & Gamble has its headquarters in Cincinnati, Ohio*. Use **its,** not *their*. And remember, *it's* is a contraction for *it is*.

13. *Who* and *whom* are always tricky. *Who* is a subject pronoun that tells who did something: *He is the man who ran the marathon. Whom* is an object pronoun that tells who received something: *The man **whom** I saw is Gary's uncle.* Gary's uncle was seen by me. He received the act of me seeing him. He was the man *whom* I saw.

15. *There* is a location. *Their* shows possession *(their book)*. The contraction for *they are* is **they're**.

Part 8 / Plurals

1. companies
2. taxes
3. bosses
4. data
5. memos
6. curricula
7. media
8. crises
9. research
10. feet

Let's review the corrections:

Plurals are not as straightforward as they may seem. Always consult a dictionary when in doubt, since a misspelled word can distract your audience from your content.

1. When the *y* is preceded by a vowel (as in *key*), just add an *s (keys)*. When the *y* is preceded by a consonant (as in *company*), change the *y* to an *i* and add *es* (**companies**).

2. Words ending in *x* require an *e* after the *x* to form a plural. Plural forms vary (oxen, **taxes**, foxes, boxes, faxes) but usually end in *s*.

3. In most cases, add *es* to words that end in *s* to avoid confusion (bosss vs. **bosses**). Some nouns ending in *s* are both plural and singular (measles, scissors, news).

4. **Data** can be used as both a singular and plural word, although the traditional singular word is *datum*.

5. Most words ending with *o* require just an *s* (**memos**, *curios, banjos, radios, pesos*), but some require an *es* (potatoes). Still others can be spelled both ways *(hobos or hoboes, dominos or dominoes)*. The safest course is to use the dictionary.

6. **Curricula** is the more common form, but *curriculums* is also acceptable.

7. **Media** is generally the plural, unless you are talking about psychic mediums.

8. Sometimes for clarity's sake, plurals require a different spelling entirely (**crises** rather than *crisises, crisisses,* or *crisiss*). If you are dealing with a singular word that has an unusual ending (*alumnus, analysis, addendum*), don't guess! Check the dictionary for the noun's plural form *(alumni, analyses, addenda)*.

9. **Research** is both a singular and plural noun. You can do *research, some research,* or *a lot of research*. But the only time you use *researches* is as a verb (*He researches his lectures thoroughly*).

10. The plural of some words does not require an *s*. The plural of *foot* is **feet**. Other examples include *goose/geese, mouse/mice,* and *man/men*.

Part 9 / Apostrophes and Commas

Let's review the corrections for apostrophes:

1. the **boy's** book (or the **boys'** book, if there is more than one boy)

2. two **months'** pay
3. the **woman's** group (or **women's** group)
4. **couldn't** make it
5. Oakland As baseball team (No apostrophe is needed with a capital letter abbreviation. You do need an apostrophe, however, with a lowercase abbreviation or letter, such as *There are two a's in the word* falafel.)

Let's review the corrections for commas:

1. Tonight Bob is cooking rice, beans, and cornbread.
2. On our trip we visited Rome and Paris and Madrid.
3. John, I know you want to go to the movies, but we don't have the money.
4. When we went to Florida, we did a lot of swimming.
5. When you write, write clearly.

1. **Two commas:** Although we punctuated this sentence with two commas, there are various styles for using commas in a series. In some cases (principally business), it is recommended that you put commas after all items in a series *(rice, beans, and cornbread)*. With other styles (principally journalism), you put commas in the series only until you reach the word *and (rice, beans and cornbread)*. Above all, it is important to select a style and stay consistent. Note: There is no comma after the word *Tonight* because it isn't needed.

2. **No commas:** The conjunction *and* is used to separate the series, so no commas are needed.

3. **Two commas:** There is a comma after the word *John*. Use a comma after addressing a person by name and/or title at the beginning of a sentence. You also use a comma after the words *no, well, yes,* or *oh* at the beginning of a sentence.

   There is a comma before the word *but*. When words such as *not, but, yet,* or *never* introduce a contradictory clause or opposing view, insert a comma in front of them: *I eat frozen yogurt, never ice cream. Joan likes to sing, but she's awful.*

4. **One comma:** Use a comma after any introductory phrase that has a verb: *When we **went** to Florida, we did a lot of swimming.* Use a comma after most introductory phrases of five words or more (this sentence has a five-word introduction).

5. **One comma:** Use a comma after any introductory phrase that has a verb. *When you **write**, write clearly.*

Let's review the corrections for quotation marks:

1. To quote the late President Franklin Roosevelt, "**We** have nothing to fear but fear **itself**."
2. "**There's** a fire in the **theater!**" screamed the usher.
3. "**Do** you have any idea what I just **said?**" he asked.
4. "**I'm afraid,**" the coach **said,** "**we're** going to have to let you **go.**"
5. "**I** Want To Hold Your **Hand**" was an early Beatles' hit.

1–3. The ending punctuation goes *inside* the quotation marks (as in . . . **itself."**) When you begin a complete sentence quote, capitalize the first word (as in "**We** have nothing to fear. . . ").

4. When a quote is interrupted, do not capitalize its second part (as in "**we're**. . .) and place commas before and after the interrupting phrase (as in. . . ,**" the** coach said, "**we're**. . .).

5. Put quote marks around song titles, book chapters, article or lecture titles, and names of poems. Notice there is no comma after the song title and before the ending quotes.

Let's review the corrections for punctuation potpourri:

All the sentences are correct, except for number 7, which should read "Do you have any idea how hard **I work out**?" she asked. Used in this context, *work out* (verb) is two words, not one, although she could have a good *workout* (noun).

Chapter Questions

1. **What is the purpose of a comma?**

   Commas are used to separate ideas or elements within a sentence.

2. **What is the purpose of an apostrophe?**

   Apsotrophes are used to show ownership, to designate contractions, and to clarify plurals.

Writing with Style

The wisecrack is a wonderful thing, and the colorful phrase, and the flight of fancy. So is the accurate description of a place or an event, and so is the precise formulation of an idea. They brighten the world.

—Edwin Newman[1]

OBJECTIVES

This chapter will help you learn:

- How to set the tone of your multimedia endeavor
- How to engage and involve your audience
- Why to choose active over passive voice
- How to keep writing lively
- How to write concise yet complete content

SET THE TONE OF YOUR MULTIMEDIA ENDEAVOR

Here are a few facts about tone in writing:

- Tone is the mood and overall character of the presentation. You set the atmosphere by setting the tone.
- Tone is determined by your subject matter and by your audience. It is extremely important to understand both *before* you craft your content.
- Tone is set by your words. Words have various connotations. Consider these two sets of words: *work, improve, tools, learn* vs. *achieve, enhance, solutions, discover.* One set of words has a school/jobs overtone while the other set has an adventure/exploration connotation.
- Tone can be conveyed with font styles and color.
- Tone helps to establish image.

Think of your own experience. How long does it take you to decide if you want to stay at a Website? What causes you to want to use some Websites and quickly leave others?

Similarly, if you sit down in a large room with other people to view a slide presentation, how long does it take you to sit up with interest or inwardly groan about having to endure the rest of it?

What causes you to form those opinions? How long does it take?

With our TV remotes and computer mouse buttons, we spend less time than ever giving a visual presentation a chance. If the subject doesn't grab us, or the information seems boring or confusing, we're gone.

Having an audience is a privilege. Having an interested audience is an accomplishment. Setting the right tone helps create and maintain that interest.

Tone Is the Mood and Overall Character of the Presentation

You set the atmosphere by setting the tone.

You just sat down with your popcorn, and the movie screen illuminates. As the opening credits appear on-screen, the music begins. Initial establishing shots introduce you to the movie's setting and some of its characters. Within the first five minutes of the movie, you know if you are about to see a plot that is scary, hilarious, warm and romantic, action-packed, or cerebral. The tone of the movie has been set for you. Your brain is engaged, your mood appropriately established, and your anticipation high (assuming it's a good movie).

As the creator of a multimedia presentation, you need to engage your viewers immediately and effectively. True, you probably don't have orchestra music, expensive sets, video action, and well-known stars to lock in your viewers' attention, but you do have other tools at your disposal. You have movement, color, fonts, sounds, images, and—most importantly—words.

Tone Is Set by Your Words

Whether you realize it or not, whatever words are spoken (or withheld) in the first five minutes of a movie are carefully crafted to bring you under the spell of the film and hold you there as the rest of the plot unfolds.

In your own multimedia presentation, words are critical to establishing viewers' interest and commitment to what you are trying to achieve. And in most cases, you have very few precious seconds to get your viewers on board.

Work hard

or

Achieve!

Improve your life

or

Enhance your life

Try our software tools

or

Try our software solutions

Learn about France

or

Discover France

In these examples, the choice of words sets the tone, even if the meaning of the words is technically the same.

Tone Is Determined by Your Subject Matter and Your Audience

It is extremely important to understand both your subject matter and your audience *before* you craft your content.

Exploration

Pretend that you have to create Websites or slide presentations on two very different subjects: New Orleans Mardi Gras, and National Bank of America.

Ask yourself these questions: How is the audience for each different? How is the tone of the subject matter different?

A good way to define the right tone is to list all the appropriate adjectives you can that fit *the subject*. As an example, go through the following list of words and match them to the subject for which they seem most appropriate—the bank or the festival:

| conservative | lighthearted | solid | dependable | festive |
| raucous | secure | noisy | stable | colorful |

Another good way to define the right tone is to list all the appropriate adjectives you can that fit *the audience*. As an example, go through the following list of words and match them to the audience for which they seem most appropriate—those interested in the bank or the festival:

| adventurous | carefree | careful | contemplative | exuberant |
| cautious | hedonistic | joyous | focused | reserved |

Even if the *same* people visit *both* sites, their moods and expectations will be different based on the subject matter. Your tone must satisfy those separate moods and expectations.

Now complete the following exercise:

1. Write a welcoming paragraph for visitors to your bank's Website and
2. Write a welcoming paragraph for visitors to your Mardi Gras Website.

The two paragraphs should be very different in tone.

Tone Can Be Conveyed with Font Styles and Color

One student of mine created a PowerPoint presentation on breast cancer awareness and used muted greens and mauves along with traditional-looking fonts. Another student did a PowerPoint presentation on her cruise to Acapulco to celebrate Carnival. Her font choices were unconventional, and her color choices ranged from pinks and reds to bright purples and blues. Both set the tone for their shows appropriately.

Tone Helps to Establish Image

Your viewers may not get to see you, so they must imagine who you are and what you are like from your words. Television commercials cast actors who project the intended tone and image, but we in multimedia must often depend on still images and our own words. Even as streaming video becomes more mainstream, it will still be words—albeit spoken words—that will have to engage viewers in just a few seconds.

Image is the concept, character, or personification you wish to project through your presentation. Your text projects image. Its mood, inflection, philosophy, appearance, and attitude influence viewers.

Recall instructors you had in school. Think of the bosses for whom you've worked. Which ones did you like? Which ones did you not like? What kind of image did they project? Were they playful, good-humored, patient, encouraging, knowledgeable, and inspiring? Were they stiff, autocratic, unimaginative, and self-absorbed? Did you find them approachable or intimidating? What gave you these impressions?

As someone who is presenting content, you hold a leadership position. You are offering information, insight, inspiration, or advice. People will form opinions about your subject matter from the words and manner you use to impart your message.

You may choose to set an honest tone and build an image that is grounded in truth. Or you can mount a flashy endeavor based entirely upon appearance. I believe that for your words to stand the test of time, you have to back them up with integrity, which requires the "three Cs"—care, consistency, and courage.

In the world of business, Lee Iacocca and Dave Thomas are cited as two leaders who sold lots of cars and burgers, respectively. In 1979, after Iacocca became chairman of Chrysler, he managed to convince the federal government to underwrite a $1.2 billion loan guarantee as well as tax concessions for the struggling car company. In addition to making a number of savvy business decisions, Iacocca became the TV pitchman for Chrysler's K-cars. Americans responded to his straightforward, gung ho message ("Lead, follow, or get out of the way") and within five years, Lee Iacocca had completely turned Chrysler around and repaid its debt. He retired in 1992 as Chrysler's chief executive.

When Dave Thomas took over as front man for his Wendy's restaurant chain in 1989, people responded immediately to his self-effacing style. Sales soared. Wearing his customary white cooking apron, the unpretentious restauranteur soon became one of the country's best-loved TV salesmen. "Dave was our patriarch, a great, big lovable man," said Jack Schuessler, chairman and CEO of Wendy's International Inc.,[2] shortly after Thomas's death in 2002. "Although Dave was widely popular, he was never very comfortable as a celebrity. He kept reminding us he was simply a hamburger cook."[3]

What did these two men exhibit that created such a positive image for their companies and products? Both came across as accessible and down-to-earth. Both projected a believable, genuine, and trustworthy image. Both acted highly knowledgeable about their products and sincerely concerned about their customers' satisfaction. People felt as if they knew these men. The men, and their products, could be counted upon. With just the right tone and image, they created a comfort zone of inclusion for potential customers.

Your challenge is to decide upon and project just the right tone and image for your Website, slide show, or other multimedia endeavor.

ENGAGE AND INVOLVE YOUR AUDIENCE

You have the right to be understood, but you have to write to be understood. Your words tell your audience who's invited and who isn't. That's why it is so important to know your audience and know for whom your content is meant.

Maybe you want to communicate with the whole world, but more realistically, you probably want to reach a particular group of viewers who can relate to your story, message, product, or idea. Find out as much as possible about your viewership. Be critically aware of the age range, background, knowledge level, interests, potential interests, biases, sensibilities, and cultures of the viewers you wish to reach. This cannot be overemphasized. As a reporter, I used to picture an imaginary group of people for whom I wrote every story. This helped remind me that I wasn't writing for a personal journal, but for people with varying views and perspectives on life.

The more you know about your audience, the better your chances for success in getting through to them. According to a predominant technology-based learning theory called Constructivism, one's beliefs and prior experiences greatly affect how new information is received and processed. Theorists believe that blending new knowledge with current conceptions and beliefs results in more lasting learning.

Helping your viewers feel welcomed and respected is essential. If they feel manipulated or insulted, they will tune you out—possibly forever. This is especially true of younger audiences who have been bombarded their entire lives by electronic media and have thus developed acute internal "hype detectors."

In a recent Inc.com article entitled "What Do Teens Want?" Blink-182 pop-punk band member Mark Hoppus, 28, noted that, "Teenagers put a lot more time and effort than the rest of us into knowing what's real. They can see what's fake right away." The article's author, David H. Freedman, elaborated:

> Hoppus believes that most businesses that target teens come off as phony, condescending, or disrespectful. "Teenagers can tell that a commercial was written by some 45-year-old guy who just wants to sell them something," he says. Instead, teens want to buy from corporations that remind them of themselves. Randomly sticking actors wearing nose rings in a chewing-gum ad won't do the trick, he warns. Instead, the best marketing efforts help companies look less like slick megacorporations and more like unpolished, offbeat underdogs, he says.[4]

(A personal aside: I have been hired to edit Websites for young audiences. I will share with you two major clues that announce when that 45-year-old guy has written a site: It has lots of exclamation points and it uses the word *cool*—a lot. *Hey kids, visit our cool toy section! See the newest cool games!*)

No matter what you write, it will go through the filters imposed by the audience. These filters include preconceived ideas, previous life experience, learning styles, core beliefs, language comprehension skills, fatigue, and many other factors. And, as much as possible, be aware that what you write is going through your *own* filters. How you view the world affects what you write.

If you aren't the right writer to connect with the intended audience:

- Hire someone who is.
- Write from your own perspective, and be honest about it. Don't try to fake it.
- Show your writing to representatives of the intended audience. Get their honest feedback. Take the feedback seriously, and don't be offended by it.

If your content is out of sync with your intended audience, you may not connect with them. Genuine communication works. Don't talk *at* viewers, but *with* them. Remember, one sentence may be enough to commit a viewer to you or turn him or her away.

Exploration

Imagine this quote on a sports-oriented Website: "He threw the ball like a girl." How might this line affect certain viewers of the Website? Who might relate to it? Who might be offended? If this line was used purposefully, who is the intended audience for the Website? Who isn't "invited"?

Imagine this quote on a cooking Website: "We all know most men can't cook, so here are some recipes even they can make." How might this line affect certain viewers of the Website? Who might relate to it? Who might be offended? If this line was used purposefully, who is the intended audience for the Website? Who isn't "invited"?

Write or discuss your opinions.

So now, let's look at some guaranteed ways to turn off viewers. Unless you are using these devices on purpose and your viewers "get it," the following things are sure to alienate your audience:

1. *Inappropriate humor.* If a subject lends itself to humor, that's fine. No sense being too serious on the "We Love Clowns" Website. But if you are writing about a somber subject such as the Holocaust or breast cancer awareness, you need to be sensitive. Just because you think something is funny doesn't mean the rest of world will laugh with you. Some sites thrive on inappropriate humor, but they know their targeted audiences expect and enjoy it.

2. *Insincere flattery and other forms of phoniness.* It is important to do a "reality check." Your viewers will. As William Shakespeare wrote in *Hamlet*, "This above all: to thine own self be true, And it must follow, as the night the day, Thou canst not then be false to any man." In multimedia writing (as in life), these are words worth considering. If we write what we know based on our own experience, knowledge, and proven instincts, the words will be far more genuine and engaging than if we try to dazzle, impress, or charm our potential viewers by writing what we think we are supposed to.

The best way to involve your audience is to involve yourself in your writing. Trust your intelligence, your likability, and your basic communication skills. After all, every day you speak to dozens of people in person or on the phone. Your writing is just one more way to share your good qualities with people who will appreciate what you have to say if you are confident in your ability to say it or if you know when to seek the input of those you trust.

3. *Pomposity and self-aggrandizement.* Don't believe your own public relations. In many cultures, a self-important braggart is little admired. In fact, the Japanese have a saying that (loosely translated) means, "The nail that sticks out gets pounded down."

4. *Disrespect.* Honor your viewers. Their time is valuable and no one has the right to abuse it. Welcome them, and don't waste their time. In addition, ignore their e-mails at your own peril. If you don't have the capacity to answer e-mails, explain that while you invite input, you cannot personally answer every e-mail. This involves creating an automatic response, which is worth doing. The best approach is to answer every e-mail individually (excluding spam). This shows users that you value their time, opinions, and business.

5. *Too many assumptions.* Define terms. Just because you know what you mean by "Optimization professional services for asset sales and financing firms" doesn't mean everyone else gets it. Never assume.

6. *Preachy tone or condescension.* How many times do you use the word *should* in your copy? Few people enjoy being lectured to or spoken down to like children. (Even children don't like it.) Your tone can be helpful and positive without "shoulding" everyone. Instead of "you should buy our products," try "please buy our products."

7. *Dullness.* If you have no enthusiasm for your content, neither will your audience. Make sure your text doesn't read like an assigned term paper, even if it involves an extremely serious, technical, or complicated topic. If you can't explain things in readily understandable terms, or if the content reads like the phone book, your audience may not care enough or may be too intimidated to hang in there.

Speaking personally, no subject baffles me more than physics. I took—and barely passed—college physics and vowed never to go near it again. I still have memories of professors droning on, using terms and examples far beyond my basis of experience.

Then, many years later, my husband introduced me to a book called *A Brief History of Time: From the Big Bang to Black Holes* by a physicist named Stephen Hawking. His ability to present great, complex theories in a way even I could (mostly) understand galvanized me as a reader, and as a writer. It reminded me that no matter what the subject, if you are knowledgeable, but also empathic and enthusiastic toward your audience, you can reach people. Consider this section on the life cycle of a star:

> A star is formed when a large amount of gas (mostly hydrogen) starts to collapse in on itself due to its gravitational attraction. As it contracts the atoms of the gas collide with each other more and more frequently and at greater and greater speeds—the gas heats up. Eventually, the gas will be so hot that when the hydrogen atoms collide they no longer bounce off each other, but instead coalesce to form helium. The heat released in this reaction, which is like a controlled hydrogen bomb explosion, is what makes the star shine. This additional heat also increases the pressure of the gas until it is sufficient to balance the gravitational attraction, and the gas stops contracting. It is a bit like a balloon—there is a balance

between the pressure of the air inside, which is trying to make the balloon expand, and the tension in the rubber, which is trying to make the balloon smaller. Stars will remain stable like this for a long time, with heat from the nuclear reactions balancing the gravitational attraction. Eventually, however, the star will run out of its hydrogen and other nuclear fuels.[5]

Hawking then goes on to explain how long our own sun may yet live and compares it with the life span of other stars. It made sense to me for the first time, and I was thrilled. And it took Professor Hawking 193 words to do it.

To me, he is not only a great physicist but also a great writer. And apparently many others agree, because the book was a huge best-seller. But what makes his writing so exceptional? The topic is complex, and he could have tried to dazzle with lots of terminology and big, fancy words. But he used simple, clear language infused with a gentle enthusiasm that makes it easy to read along. He also uses examples, explaining stars in comparison to nuclear bombs and balloons. And it worked for me because I can relate to these things (I prefer relating to balloons).

8. *General stuffiness.* You have my official blessing never to use the words *hence, therefore, furthermore, wherewithal, notwithstanding, whereas, forthwith, aforementioned,* or *wherein* in any multimedia presentation!

9. *Clichés.* Hackneyed, tired writing is the bane of creativity. I roll my eyes every time I am forced to read expressions such as *win-win, think outside the box, move forward, drill down,* or *buckle down.* Such expressions are readily understood by the cultures from which they spring (in this case, the Western business culture), but that doesn't mean they are being well received. Tired expressions that are used too often are likely to provoke derision within their culture of origin. As for anyone not familiar with that particular culture, the clichés may not be clear at all.

10. *Cold, distant demeanor.* Speak directly with your audience, and engage them with a warm, conversational tone. Compare these two paragraphs:

> "We'd like to welcome you to our Website about male pattern baldness. Thank you for stopping by. We'll try to answer your questions and guide you toward effective solutions."

> "This Website was prepared to address the issue of male pattern baldness. It will detail many of the medical and emotional aspects of this condition for people who are suffering from its effects."

I think you'll agree that the first paragraph sounds more as if the writers genuinely care and understand.

11. *Insisting on perfection.* Everyone has flaws and makes mistakes. Not being willing to admit them creates resentment and mistrust. Newspapers run

Exploration

Rewrite this paragraph in a way that sounds "real" to you. Reach out to your audience warmly and genuinely. Rid this text of all the turnoffs mentioned above. There is no one right way to fix this text, but you can visit page 124 to see one example of how it could be helped. Try it yourself first! You can do it.

> Do you have the wherewithal to improve your present circumstance? No matter what one's age, one should be thinking about the ramifications of inadequate preparation for the retirement years. Most people allow ignorance and procrastination to dissuade them from their long-term financial responsibilities. Our excellent book *Retire in Complete Comfort* provides without a doubt the single best analysis to date of what the digerati of finance have overwhelmingly described as the coming crisis. Everyone should use this book to examine the political, economic, and social dimensions of collective inaction. This book will provide even the most ill prepared with much-needed enlightenment and an incentive toward reformation.

clarifications and corrections routinely to maintain their credibility with readers. Websites must have the same policy. Provide clarifications or correct inaccurate copy immediately.

CHOOSE ACTIVE OVER PASSIVE VOICE

There are two primary aspects to using active voice. One involves the way you address the audience. As you may have noticed throughout this book, I am writing directly to *you*.

By using pronouns such as *I, me, my, mine, ours, you, your, yours, we,* and *us,* you can make your communication feel more direct, more person-to-person. You don't have to use the word *you* in every sentence to establish that one-to-one feeling. Sometimes the word *you* is understood. See what I mean? (*Can you* is understood, as in "*Can you* see what I mean?") When you use pronouns such as *one, they, them, he, she, it, oneself, anybody,* and *whomever,* the communication feels more indirect and less personal. Many nouns such as *people, students,* and *teachers* can also create this effect.

Multimedia lends itself to a warmer and more direct writing style. Plus, multimedia writers generally have less time to establish a rapport with the audience than writers for newspapers, magazines, and other printed media; so building a sense of immediacy with viewers becomes very important.

Exploration

Rewrite these sentences to make them more direct and personal. Possible solutions can be found on page 124.

1. When choosing a puppy, it is important to know the breed's temperament.
2. One must understand how much, how often, and what to feed a puppy.
3. People should know where the puppy came from and avoid "puppy mills."
4. Others need to be patient when they try to housebreak a puppy.
5. It can be fun if the new owner is fully prepared.

The second aspect of active voice involves the verb. Active verb usage is more direct and engaging than passive constructions. The easiest way to explain it for our purposes is this: If you use *was* or *were* in a sentence so that the subject receives the verb's action rather than doing the action, you've made it passive. Try not to write sentences that are passive, unless you're delivering criticism or bad news.

Let's look at some examples.

Passive	A breakthrough *was* discovered in skin care.
Active	We discovered a breakthrough in skin care.
Passive	A decisive battle *was* fought yesterday.
Active	Soldiers fought a decisive battle yesterday.
Passive	Two reports on the new school addition *were* presented.
Active	Stan presented two reports on the new school addition.

Here are some advantages of active voice over passive voice in multimedia:

1. It sounds more immediate, concise, and direct—the essence of multimedia (in contrast to traditional print media that can be more staid, contemplative, analytical, lengthy, and permanent).
2. It may require fewer words—another plus in multimedia writing.
3. It's clearer, cleaner, and easier to comprehend quickly—a third plus when people are trying to read text on a screen rather than on paper.

This is **not** to imply that passive voice is always inappropriate, particularly if you have the task of delivering bad news or criticism. But the choice to use passive voice must be a conscious one that suits your communication objectives. Passive is more indirect and subtle, especially when the news isn't good.

For example, if a Website has a page announcing a major recall of one of its products, it might be preferable to write "Fourteen thousand defective widgets produced by our company were named in a recall order issued last week by government officials" rather than "The government says 14,000 of our widgets are defective, so send them back." The second sentence is certainly more active and shorter, but a softer touch may be more appropriate considering the content.

Likewise, it is probably preferable to write "An unexpected drop in the company's stock price has occurred" rather than "Our company's stock has tanked!" Both tell the truth, but the first—in passive voice—is less jolting.

Exploration

Change these sentences from passive to active voice. Possible answers appear on page 124.

1. The emancipation of America from England was announced by the Declaration of Independence.
2. It was a proclamation written by the Second Continental Congress.
3. The Congress was made up of representatives from all 13 original colonies.
4. America's independence from Great Britain was declared by the proclamation.
5. A war was started after the document was ratified on July 4, 1776.

Sometimes you want to use an approach that establishes more formality. Here are some ways to accomplish that:

Formal	*Informal*
Use third-person (customer):	Use second-person (you):
"The customer is always right."	*"You are always right."*
Avoid contractions:	Use contractions:
Do not bend the corners.	*Don't bend the corners.*

KEEP WRITING LIVELY

Traditional print-based writing has the luxury of going in-depth, presenting elaborate phrasing, and displaying long, involved sentences and paragraphs (like this one). In multimedia writing, such text just looks clunky. And writing that works in print can *sound* clunky in a multimedia setting, too.

Multimedia is about action, movement, immediacy, and evolution. To be effective, writing must reflect the medium.

Compare the following sets of sentences. Decide which statement in each group sounds livelier, more immediate, more interesting:

Learn about the country of Mexico.

Explore Mexico.

Take a cooking lesson and make some lasagna.

Create savory lasagna.

Understand the classical music of Bach.

Get Bach.

Read about archaeology.

Dig the past.

Get a degree in fashion design so you can go to work.

Fashion your destiny.

The *second* clause in each group is better geared to a multimedia audience in part because of the use of "power verbs." Verbs such as *discover, master, unleash, dig, explore,* and *challenge* extend a special energy and power to the writing. Verbs such as *learn, read, understand, comprehend, check,* and *acquire* are OK to use, but they have a drier business or schoolroom feel. They are not power verbs. "Begin today" sounds less immediate and active than "Start now."

Power verbs make you want to start, move, seek, enjoy, expand, and grow. They come with their own excitement and imagery that is always action oriented. Even when you are writing titles for a navigation bar, try to use power verbs. Don't put "Our Online Store" on your navigation bar; put "Buy the Best!" or "Shop for Bargains." Energize your viewers so they *want* to visit your Web pages.

WRITE CONCISE YET COMPLETE CONTENT

The second statement in each group above is geared to a multimedia audience for two other reasons: subtle but appropriate humor, and brevity. Meaning is not lost because there are fewer words; in fact, it is enhanced. Being concise is a key component of effective multimedia writing. Less really can be more.

Exploration

The following sentences are convoluted versions of common clichés. Try to figure out the simplified versions. You'll find possible answers on page 125, but your approach may be better!

1. You shouldn't rush through the tasks at hand because you are apt to make mistakes.
2. If you're feeling really positive about life, you might want to demonstrate it now by putting your hands together and applauding.
3. What gives us the most satisfaction in life doesn't cost any money.
4. I would suggest at this moment that you cease and desist from your present course of action.
5. In the interest of time, let us entertain an adjournment for the purposes of a brief gastronomical repast.

When you write a novel, you can create as many pages as you want. But when you write for multimedia, your text must be more succinct and much crisper. A primary reason for this is because it is harder to read text on a screen than it is to read text on paper.

If you are using multimedia as your source of communication, then you must write for that medium. In some ways, it is much harder to write for multimedia than for print. You have to choose your words carefully because you do not have the luxury of using as many words as you may wish. It is the difference between writing a scientific tome on endangered tigers and writing a zoo exhibit sign. In the late 1980s, I was hired to do just that for the San Diego Zoo. I spent hours interviewing zookeepers, reading about tigers, and observing them in their enclosures. Then I had to boil down everything I had learned into one sign. The sign had to capture the attention of passing zoo visitors and give them vital information about the status of tigers in the wild. I could have written a book. Instead, I wrote one sign.

Amazingly, it was one of the hardest writing assignments I ever had, but it prepared me for multimedia writing a few years later. Based on my experience, here are a few important tips for multimedia writers:

- Choose your focus carefully.
- Limit what you plan to cover.
- Answer the *who, what, where, when,* and *why* in as few words as possible, being careful not to exclude any vital details.

Remember that it is possible to be concise without being complete. Baseball legend Yogi Berra is known as a master of being concise without being complete. He is famous for almost presenting useful information. Here is my favorite Yogi-ism: "If you come to a fork in the road, take it."[6] Concise, yes; complete, no. But the lovable Hall of Fame catcher, manager, and coach can get away with it. Those of us trying to communicate in the multimedia world can't.

Review

1. Tone is determined by your subject matter and by your audience. It is extremely important to understand both *before* you craft your content.
2. Tone is also established with font styles and color.
3. Tone helps to establish image.
4. Your text projects image. Its mood, inflection, philosophy, appearance, and attitude influence viewers.
5. As someone who is presenting content, you hold a leadership position. You are offering information, insight, inspiration, or advice.
6. People will form opinions about your subject matter from the words and manner you use to impart your message.
7. For your words to stand the test of time, you have to back them up with integrity, which requires the "three Cs"—care, consistency, and courage.
8. Your words tell your audience who's invited and who isn't. That's why it is so important to know your audience and know for whom your content is meant.
9. You have the right to be understood, but you have to write to be understood.
10. Be critically aware of the age range, background, knowledge level, interests, potential interests, biases, sensibilities, and cultures of the viewers you wish to reach.
11. According to a predominant technology-based learning theory called Constructivism, one's beliefs and prior experiences greatly affect how new information is received and processed.
12. No matter what you write, it will go through the filters imposed by the audience. These filters include preconceived ideas, previous life experience, learning styles, core beliefs, language comprehension skills, fatigue, and many other factors.
13. What you write is going through your *own* filters. How you view the world affects what you write.
14. If you aren't the right writer to connect with the intended audience, hire someone who is; write from your own perspective, and be honest about it; or show your writing to representatives of the intended audience for their honest feedback.

15. Genuine communication works. Don't talk *at* viewers, but *with* them.
16. Power verbs make you want to start, move, seek, enjoy, expand, and grow. They come with their own excitement and imagery that is always action oriented.

Key Terms and Concepts

Image The concept, character, or personification you wish to project through your presentation.

Tone The mood and overall character of the presentation.

Chapter Questions

1. What are 10 guaranteed ways to turn off viewers?
2. What are two primary aspects of active voice?
3. What are three advantages of active voice over passive voice in multimedia?

Now You Try

On the CD-ROM, visit the recommended Helpful Websites for Chapter 6 to find:

- Differences between paper and online presentations
- Tips on writing quality content for business-oriented Websites

Write 15 interesting facts you learned from visiting these Websites. Identify where each fact came from (by Website title and Web page address).

Endnotes

1. Newman, E. (1975). *Strictly speaking: Will America be the death of English?* New York: Warner Books.
2. *Wendy's founder dead at 69.* (2002, January 8). CNNMoney [Online]. money.cnn.com/2002/01/08/companies/wendys_obit
3. Ibid.
4. Freedman, D. H. (2000, December 1). What Do Teens Want? *Inc* magazine [Online]. inc.com/incmagazine. Retrieved from

www.inc.com/articles/marketing/market_research/demographics/
21117.html

5. Hawking, S. (1988–90). *A brief history of time: From the big bang to black holes.* New York: Bantam Books.

6. Berra, Y. (1998). *The Yogi book.* New York: Workman Publishing.

Answers for Chapter 6

Exploration

Below is one suggested revision of the paragraph on page 117. Note that the original paragraph consisted of 106 words, while the revised paragraph below has only 74.

> Do you know how to improve your financial health? No matter how old you are, it's a good idea to plan ahead. Don't be like others, who fail to understand or even try to learn how to have secure, happy retirements. Our excellent book *Retire in Complete Comfort* explains why the world is headed for financial crisis and how you can avoid it. Get prepared to survive and even thrive in tough economic times.

Exploration

Here are some possible solutions to the exercise on page 118.

1. Know the breed's temperament before choosing your puppy.
2. Understand how much, how often, and what to feed your puppy.
3. Make sure your puppy came from a reputable breeder.
4. Housebreaking a puppy requires patience.
5. You'll have fun if you're prepared.

Exploration

Below are possible answers to the exercise on page 119.

1. The Declaration of Independence freed America from England.
2. The Second Continental Congress drafted the proclamation.
3. Originally, Congress consisted of representatives from 13 colonies.
4. The proclamation declared America's freedom from Great Britain.
5. War started after the document was ratified on July 4, 1776.

Exploration

Here are possible answers to the exercise on page 121.

1. Haste makes waste.
2. If you're happy and you know it, clap your hands.
3. The best things in life are free.
4. Stop it.
5. Let's break for lunch.

Chapter Questions

1. **What are 10 guaranteed ways to turn off viewers?** *(Here are all 11.)*

1. Inappropriate humor
2. Insincere flattery and other forms of phoniness
3. Pomposity and self-aggrandizement
4. Disrespect
5. Too many assumptions
6. Preachy tone or condescension
7. Dullness
8. General stuffiness
9. Clichés
10. Cold, distant demeanor
11. Insisting on perfection

2. **What are two primary aspects of using active voice?**

One involves the way you address the audience. The second aspect of active voice involves the verb; active verb usage is more direct and engaging.

3. **What are three advantages of active voice over passive voice in multimedia?**

1. It sounds more immediate, concise, and direct—the essence of multimedia.
2. It may require fewer words.
3. It's clearer, cleaner, and easier to comprehend quickly—a third plus when people are trying to read text on a screen rather than on paper.

Words as Graphic Elements

A word is not a crystal, transparent and unchanged; it is the skin of a living thought, and may vary greatly in color and content according to the circumstances and the time in which it is used.

—Oliver Wendell Holmes, opinion, *Towne v. Eisner*, January 7, 1918

OBJECTIVES

This chapter will help you learn:

- The evolution and revolution of words
- To use font styles and sizes effectively
- To add color to text for special effect
- To understand how contrast and movement impact text
- To explore other emphasis techniques and monitor their use

There is an old joke that goes, "What's black and white and *red* all over?" The answer is a newspaper, which is black and white and *read* all over. Well, that joke certainly doesn't apply to multimedia, which is anything but black and white—although hopefully your efforts will be *read* all over because they are so captivating!

We are in the midst of the latest revolution in words. They are now visual elements as well as textual ones. Consider this course description for an *art* class at San Francisco State University:

Art 511.× Digital Word and Image

A studio course in the tools of desktop publishing, digital photography, conceptual arts, the exploration of information as aesthetic material and a critical analysis of corporate advertising. No prerequisites.

Because of multimedia, information has become art.

THE EVOLUTION AND REVOLUTION OF WORDS

Three things in history have largely affected the viewing and mass dissemination of words. First came paper, perfected around A.D. 100 by the Chinese. This was a breakthrough because it allowed people to view words, but it wasn't very efficient for mass dissemination. For the most part, scribes painstakingly handwrote the majority of documents made available to the world. There were even shops called scriptoria where you could hire someone to write your words down on paper (a long and expensive process).

Secondly, some 1,300 years after paper made its debut, German businessman Johannes Gutenberg invented the printing press. This revolutionized the aesthetics of words, introducing the clustering of words and various letter sizes, rather than evenly spaced written letters. Gutenberg's printed Latin Bible became the first best-seller and eventually led to others developing printing presses of their own, much to the dismay of religious leaders, who had previously controlled most of what got disseminated to the masses. (It was rather like the founding of the Internet, which has caused some in control of mass media to bemoan how words are now the purview of any plebeian with a Website!)

Over time and after much trial and error, standards for displaying text were established. Innovations such as setting headlines and placing text in neat columns became the rage.

In fact, until the mid-twentieth century, words lived pretty much a black-and-white existence—black ink on white paper, that is. Text was confined to regimented columns. Putting colored text or other fancy word effects into a printed publication cost more money—sometimes a lot more money—so doing anything unusual with text required financial justification.

As a former newspaper reporter, I can remember the great excitement back in the 1970s when newspapers began to use colored ink for photos on their front pages—and this had little to do with changing the look of text. Text remained encased in its black-and-white world, constricted inside rows, columns, and paragraphs as it had been for 600 years. The technology for printing had improved, but not to the extent that it impacted text display very much.

But then came the third thing that changed the life of words. It was the personal computer. What followed were color printers, the Internet, and multimedia presentation software, which now make it possible to enliven words with lots of colors, sizes, shapes, and even sound effects and movement.

Best of all, none of these special text effects costs more money! Rather than words being printed, they can now be displayed on screens.

So congratulations! You are currently part of the newest revolution to define how language should look. It's an exciting time in history for anyone who works with words. Text is jumping off the printed page and into cyberspace. New standards are emerging for how text should appear on-screen.

And indirectly (especially with the advent of desktop publishing software), those rules are beginning to affect how text appears on paper. After all, if you can see words come to life with color and vibrancy on-screen, why should you settle for them looking dull on paper?

And how will the publishing world come to terms with its presentation of electronic books? Will they be black-and-white text-based presentations on a screen? Or will electronic books continue to evolve into dynamic yet easy-to-read print-meets-multimedia text displays? Right now, a chief complaint among some who read electronic books is that the presentation bothers their eyes. Could it be because traditional text presentation doesn't work that well on-screen?

I keep busy these days as a writer, editor, and multimedia instructor teaching students and consulting with news- and businesspeople. I can tell pretty quickly when viewing a Website, slide presentation, or any other visual arena for words (such as the TV screen) if its creators gave the appearance of words much thought. If the text is too bland, too small, too crowded, or too traditionally print oriented, I know the answer is, "No. We're doing what's always been done in the past." If the text is too garish, too large, too incomplete, or too hyperkinetic (endlessly flashing at me or flooding by in a steady stream across the bottom of the screen), I know the answer is, "Yes. We're using every multimedia trick available, and not well." If the text is easy to read, not crowded, not overwhelmed with special effects, and lively and original, I know the answer is, "We get it. We understand multimedia writing, and we know what we're doing."

> *"Fancy media on websites typically fails user testing. Simple text and clear photos not only communicate better with users, they also enhance users' feeling of control and thus support the Web's mission as an instant gratification environment."[1]*
>
> —Jakob Nielsen

Speaking as someone who has spent my entire career as a professional writer (and as a multimedia writer since 1994), I maintain that in addition to writing great words, you have to think *carefully* about "costuming" them.

If you overuse special effects such as word movement, you detract from what you are trying to say. Unless you use these devices on purpose, they may not serve you well. The object for most writers is to achieve clarity, not to overwhelm or confuse people.

With every sentence you create as a multimedia writer, you must ask yourself if that sentence really needs to stand out somehow.

- Does it need to draw extra attention?
- Is it more important than the other sentences you have written?
- Does it introduce other sentences?
- Is it an important summary statement?
- Does it deserve its own special effect?
- If so, just what kind of special effect?
- How much is too much?

Used correctly, special effects—or emphasis—can help you really drive home a point. Emphasis can draw attention to words, thoughts, and phrases you consider very important. Emphasis tells your viewer where to look first. It announces which sentences, phrases, and words you consider most important, and/or the place to start.

Like casting actors in a play, you can decide which of your words deserve the leading role and which are supporting players (unless, of course, you are attempting to stage a mob scene of words).

USE FONT STYLES AND SIZES EFFECTIVELY

When writing for traditional print media, selecting a font may not be that big a deal. Usually Arial, Times New Roman, or Helvetica will do just fine. They are standard type fonts for letters, memos, and other printed material.

But in the world of multimedia, font choices can impact the mood of your presentation. Remember, words are now part of the overall design, so if you are doing a lighthearted topic for children, you might want to go with a childlike font such as Felt Tip.

For a very historic or traditional topic, consider formal headlines set in or Old English Text. As you can see, the choice of a font sets a mood for your topic, so select your fonts with care. (By the way, combining fonts that do not harmonize—such as Felt Tip with Old English Text—can offend your viewers' sense of aesthetics.)

In terms of a Website, your font choices are somewhat limited (at least for now), in part because fonts weren't a high priority in early versions of HTML (hypertext markup language). That's changing now, as the importance of text finally gets due recognition. So you have more opportunity to choose specialty fonts. Remember, though, that your visitors who do not have the same fonts on their computers may see a default font instead, such as good old Arial, Times New Roman, or Helvetica.

If you are really determined to keep your font choice, you can post an actual document on your Website that you first create using a word-processing program, then it will display the same way a photo would display, as a single element. You can't edit it online, however. By creating custom text as a graphic file, you do lose scalability. Such text will always appear on-screen in the same size it was created. This approach is most useful for headers, logos, or the combination of text with images or graphic elements.

You can also employ more special effects, such as drop shadowing, by using text as a pre-created graphics file. There are software programs that can make customized graphics-based text. Macromedia (www.macromedia.com) offers various software programs to help you, including Fontographer and Flash.

Serif or Sans Serif Fonts

Print-based studies have suggested that sans serif fonts (fonts without little tails such as **Helvetica Bold** or **Arial**) are harder to read because the letters do not flow from one to the next. (The word *sans* is French for without). Yet many Web designers prefer them because they don't blur or run together, which is important in light of the decreased resolution available on a computer screen. In fact, sans serif fonts are the norm for streaming video. Because viewing text on-screen is harder than reading it on paper, letters that don't run together are often easier to discern.

Serif fonts are easier to read in print because they have tails that lead directly to the next letter. Some examples of serif fonts (think of them as the equivalent of cursive handwriting as opposed to printing) include **Times New Roman** and **Century**. Note how the "a" in the Times font has a little tail. Serif fonts (notably Times, Bodoni, and Baskerville) are generally considered more elegant than sans serif fonts . But sans serif fonts are considered more "hip" and project a more modern feel.

Sizing Up Your Words

There is really no hard and fast rule when it comes to font sizes, but remember that various fonts appear larger or smaller even though they may technically be the same size. A 12-point Helvetica bold font appears larger than a 12-point Palatino font.

Here's 12-point Helvetica Bold.
Here's 12-point Palatino.

Older and younger users prefer larger type, perhaps even 14 points, on Websites. For slide shows, I never use any font size smaller than 28 points.

Multimedia writers and editors would do well to take a typography class to learn about various fonts (or typefaces), how to size them, and how to arrange them professionally on a site (through techniques such as leading and kerning).

In terms of a visual presentation, remember that not all computers have the same fonts, so if you create a slide show or Web page on one computer, you might be surprised later when a lot of ordinary-looking default fonts pop up in the middle of your beautifully designed show or page. This happens because the computer that displays your presentation or Web page must be programmed with the same fonts in order for them to show up.

You can't do much to control all the computers in the world that might display your Website, so be careful if you pick an unusual novelty font. Try viewing your Website on various computers with different operating systems to get an idea of what your words might look like.

If you are giving a slide presentation, try to rehearse on the machine you will be using to check the fonts ahead of time. See if the fonts in your presentation are programmed on the machine you will be using. Otherwise, the computer might pick default fonts for you that are much too large or small for the screen. Better that you fix font problems ahead of time than be surprised in front of an audience.

Exploration

Visit the Web, and search for three Websites that use fonts to set the right mood. Remember that the fonts will probably be graphic elements in GIF format, rather than basic paragraphed text (such as Arial, Times New Roman, or Helvetica, which are the Web's default fonts). Try to find:

- A lighthearted, fun Website with playful fonts
- A serious, stalwart Website with strong, conservative fonts
- An adventure-based or sports Website with wild, exaggerated fonts

Notice how the topic headings in this chapter are larger than the rest of the text. They stand out more. They indicate that a new subject area is about to be covered.

Bigger words tend to get noticed before smaller words. Bigger text says, "This is important; look here first." Bigger text adds emphasis or gives viewers direction in terms of where to look first. The default font sizes used in computer systems (10 point, 12 point, etc.) represent common sizes of typewritten text or printed typography. For example, 12-point font is standard for most business letters.

When computers were mainly word-processing machines, standard fonts worked well. But with the development of Websites and slide presentations, the computer screen itself—rather than paper—is often the destination point for words. So type size is taking on a more varied (and unpredictable) role, especially since different computer platforms, operating systems, and screen sizes display fonts differently. In Web browsers, there are default font types and sizes to use as starting points, but these can be changed by the Web page designer or by the Web page user to display text at a larger or smaller size on the particular machine they are using.

It is definitely worth taking a beginning HTML class to learn the proper ways to display and size text. If, for example, you wish to make sections of text larger or smaller, Web markup language lets you use "relative font sizing" (noted as "+1," "+2," or "−1," "−2," etc.). Web browsers tend to default to business-letter type size and very basic font style (say, 12-point Helvetica) unless you have coded something different. If a browser reads your coding as "−1," it would display one size smaller (10-point Helvetica).

There are also header, or title, sizes. Header 1 is the largest-size text and Header 6 is the smallest. Headers are used for titles.

Here's Header 1.

Here's Header 4.

Here's normal text.

You would use H2 to indicate a subsection of H1, and so on down the line. Headers are not meant to be used as special effects. If you use the "header" tag for the title of a section and a font-size tag for the title of a same-size section at a later point, spacing and font size may be different between the two subject headings. So it's important to be consistent when coding.

How should you determine the size of your text? Look at the front page of any newspaper. The biggest headline is shouting, "Read me first!" Editors sit in daily meetings to decide which story is most important and deserves the biggest headline. Notice how the headlines tend to get smaller as your eyes move down the page. These stories have been judged to be second, third, and so on in importance.

This prioritizing gives text *weight*. Giving text weight is a conscious decision you make in terms of how and where to place text. In a well-designed Website or presentation, you decide what you want your viewers to read first, second, third, and so forth. Many times, a Website visitor will complain that a page is confusing. This is often because all the text and pictures have the same weight. By varying text size, you give viewers important visual cues that help them get their bearings and not feel confused.

Never use a font size that is too small. While 12-point type is great for business letters, it may prove hard to read on a Website, especially if viewers are particularly old or young. Don't be afraid to bump up text size a notch, particularly if you are trying to attract viewers who are over 40 years old (smaller type gets harder to read as we age). When producing slide shows for an average-size room or larger, try to avoid using fonts smaller than 28 points (or the equivalent) because they cannot be easily read on a projector screen.

Researcher Bob Bailey, Ph.D., chief scientist for Human Factors International, evaluated research conducted on font styles and sizes related to the Web. He concluded the following:

- No Web page fonts should be less than 10-points.
- Optimal reading speed for most adults will be elicited with 12-point fonts (size = 3).
- There is probably no reliable difference in reading speed for most adults when viewing common font styles (Arial, Verdana, Georgia, Times New Roman).
- Most users tend to prefer sans serif fonts (Arial, Verdana).
- Older users will benefit from type sizes that are at least 14-points.[2]

ADD COLOR TO TEXT FOR SPECIAL EFFECT

Another way to bring emphasis to text is to make your words colorful (literally!) Color needs to be used deliberately, whether you're creating a visual presentation or a Web page. Don't use too many colors, or colors that aren't pleasing together unless you do it on purpose.

"With the growing impact of global communication, the importance of color and its influence on modern life has never been so evident. No business or individual can afford to be color unaware."[3]
—Color Association of the United States

If you plan to write for multimedia on a regular basis, it is a good idea to take a basic art class where you can learn about color principles and aesthetics. But for our purposes, let's do a quick review of what many of us learned back in elementary school.

The basic 12 colors are displayed on a color wheel. (See the inside back cover for a color wheel.) The three primary colors are yellow, red, and blue. You make secondary colors (orange, purple, and green) by mixing two primaries. Yellow and red make orange. Red and blue make purple. Blue and yellow make green.

The other six colors on the color wheel are called tertiaries. Mixing a primary and secondary color together creates them. Colors on the wheel are either complementary, analogous, or triadic.

Complementary colors lie directly across the color wheel from one another (for example, blue and orange or red and green). Analogous colors are any three adjacent colors (for example, blue-violet, blue, and blue-green). You get a harmonious feeling from analogous compositions because the colors contain common traits. Lastly, there are triadic colors, which are equidistant (for example, red, yellow, and blue). Because of their relationship around the color wheel, triadic colors seem very balanced.

Colors please or displease us because of psychological and cultural cues we attach to them. Some color psychology theories contend to varying degrees that we are comfortable with colors based on our primal associations with nature and survival. Blues and greens are interpreted as restful or peaceful, as are blue skies, still waters, and green, leafy shade trees. Reds and oranges, on the other hand, attract immediate attention because of our primal associations with survival: warm campfires, the color of fruit sought by foraging ancestors, the color of blood, fire trucks.

There are also deep cultural connections to colors, which are particularly important to remember when you are producing text for a Website. Since a worldwide audience can view Websites, consider cultural sensitivities and symbolism if you don't want to offend international visitors. Neutral tones (brown, gray, black) are usually safest for text.

We have many subtle associations with colors we may not even realize. In America, teachers often use red ink to grade papers, making red text a sign of authority and correction. Blue is considered a strong, masculine color. Pink is often seen as feminine. Consider that IBM is referred to as Big Blue, and Mattel's Barbie is marketed in pink.

In one of my classes I watched a group of teenage boys visit a Website that had a pink background. They immediately assumed it was meant for girls and clicked out of it. (By the way, it *was* a site meant for girls.)

When using color in a multimedia presentation, there are also practical considerations. How colors appear on the Web or on different computers can depend on what kind of computer a viewer is using, what color settings are programmed on that computer, and what browser is being used. So check out your text on different kinds of computers if possible. For Websites, try to stick with "Web-safe" colors, which are 216 colors programmed to look the same on any computer using any Web browser. (A chart of these colors appears on the inside back cover of this book.)

Always go for contrast—light font on a dark background or dark font on a light background—because it makes words easier to read on-screen. Even if a color combination looks good on your computer monitor, if you plan to show it on a projector screen, you will lose a lot of resolution. The best advice is to try to see what the text looks like before projecting your presentation to an audience.

Exploration

What are your two favorite colors? Explain why these are your favorites.

Visit the color wheel at the companion Website, and see how these colors correspond on the color wheel. Are they complementary, analogous, or triadic? Or do they seem not to fit any pattern at all?

Is there a color you absolutely hate? Why?

For fun, try the online Color Quiz at www.colorquiz.com.

UNDERSTAND HOW CONTRAST AND MOVEMENT IMPACT TEXT

Lights, camera, action!

Words are no longer static entities lying on a page. They can move and appear with background sounds courtesy of current software programs for both Websites and presentations.

While it may be tempting to add sound effects and movements to words, ask yourself if such emphasis enhances or detracts from what you are trying to say. In the case of a visual presentation, you will probably be talking while your slides are projecting. And it can be very difficult to talk over the constant sound of explosions, typewriter clicks, or other noises. Use a sound only for the effect of drawing attention to a specific thing. And don't forget that people have to adjust their eyes to movements on-screen, which makes reading text harder.

A sound or movement can bring drama to text if properly and thoughtfully placed. Otherwise, it can just become an annoying distraction. Studies have established that the eye is initially drawn to motion, but that motion does not promote focus or concentration and can quickly become distracting. So use movement purposefully and sparingly—only for a quick, attention-grabbing effect. Then turn it off!

EXPLORE OTHER EMPHASIS TECHNIQUES AND MONITOR THEIR USE

If a Web page or slide is said to be "too gray," that means it looks too text-heavy. Viewers tend not to want to wade through a massive block of gray text on a screen, even though they might not think twice about reading the same number of words on paper.

Think about this from your own experience. If you get a two-page letter in the mail, you probably don't mind reading it. But if you get a two-page e-mail that requires you to scroll and scroll and scroll, you might not want to finish it.

Viewers are likely to react the same way if they feel bombarded by too many words on a screen. So if you are dealing with a lot of text (say, a long news article or an annual report), you can break it up visually by using emphasis techniques. Some simple emphasis techniques include:

- <u>underlining text</u> (avoid on Websites because it looks like a hyperlink)
- *putting text in italics*
- changing a portion of text to a different font
- **putting text in boldface**
- putting text in a box.

If you choose any of these techniques use them in a consistent pattern, so they don't just add confusion. For example, this book presents subheads all set in the same larger type size and boldfaced. This pattern helps break up text, introduce new sections, and provide visual order.

Be careful about USING ALL CAPS as an emphasis technique. While it can be effective for headlines, it tends to "scream" at viewers (which is why it is considered rude to use all caps when writing e-mails, unless you are REALLY ANGRY).

One final caution: If emphasis techniques are overused, they can trivialize your text and the credibility of your words, reducing even the best-constructed copy to the level of a child's coloring book. The same holds true for information you may wish to impart through a chart or graph. Don't pick bright colors just because they are interesting or have a lot of contrast. Colors chosen for information in charts and graphs can actually confuse viewers if they have no apparent rhyme or reason.

There is a whole science devoted to designing charts and graphs. And while designers and graphic artists are generally taught these principles, writers tend to think about the information first and the science of displaying it second (if at all). Business presentations and Websites may feature graphs and charts put together by people with no training or background at all other than a knowledge of how to use the software that makes charts!

Here are three concepts to consider the next time you decide to create a graph or chart to dramatize facts or information:

1. When you choose a color for a portion of a graph, ask yourself why. Since people tend to notice brighter, bolder colors first, associate those colors with what you consider the most important information—the information you want viewers to notice first or most easily.

2. Too many bright or gaudy colors cause the viewer to lose focus. It becomes hard to understand what you are trying to emphasize if the bright orange bar graph line is placed next to the bright red bar graph line.

3. Try to create as much contrast between findings as possible. Look at the pie chart in Figure 7.1. Can you see much difference between the rats and cats sections? Neither can other viewers. Now look at the pie chart in Figure 7.2, where dogs are delineated in black and bats are delineated in white. Isn't it easier to quickly see the difference between the sections? If a chart or graph is too hard to decipher within a few seconds, many viewers will skip it.

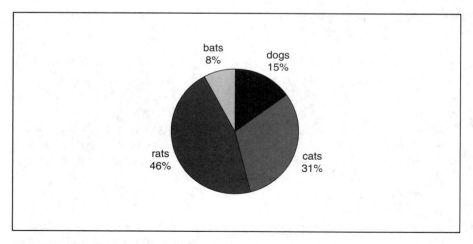

FIGURE 7.1   Pie chart with ineffective contrast.

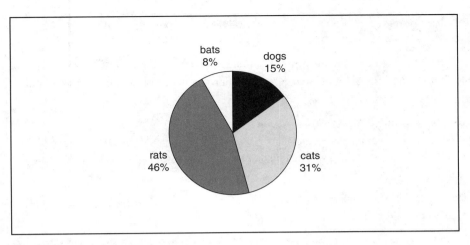

FIGURE 7.2 Pie chart with effective contrast.

Exploration

Are TV Networks Getting It Right?

When I received my B.A. in telecommunications (with a special emphasis in broadcasting) in the early 1970s, no one encouraged us to add a lot of words to the television screen. Less was more. Words were spoken. Words that appeared on the screen generally reinforced a concept, introduced a product or person's name, or provided contact information. Words also appeared in credits before and after a TV show. But they never took center stage or competed with the visuals.

Now, however, it is not uncommon to have a TV anchorperson reading text off a TelePrompTer while completely different text marches like determined ants across the bottom of the TV screen. At the same time, there may also be multiple screens, text boxes, flashing sports scores, spinning logos, title graphics, and a moving ticker tape of stock prices.

Industry insiders claim the concept appeals to their primary target audience—that is, younger viewers with shorter attention spans who are used to multitasking on computer screens. They even acknowledge that "older viewers" or newer computer users might not like the concept.

Those of us trained to effectively blend words and visuals into a seamless multimedia environment think the jury is still out on the overall communicative effectiveness of all this lively "eye candy" (to quote an industry term).

What do you think: is it "eye candy" or "eye clutter"?

Exploration

Below is a July 18, 2001, news article from the Associated Press news service. Read the article thoroughly. Determine your point of view. Has this been a positive or negative trend in multimedia writing? Why or why not?

All the News That Fits: Read Any Good Television Lately?

The volume of on-screen information will increase in the next two months when new versions of CNN Headline News and ESPNews are launched as part of the transformation of TV viewing in the computer age.

CNN Headline News will include business news, headlines and a weather map in an expanded display that will leave only about half of the TV picture for news anchors, starting Aug. 6.

On Sept. 7, sports channel ESPNews will move from a single line of scores to a larger band that also includes game updates and news items.

Network logos, small and relatively discreet, were in the vanguard of on-screen data. Now, broadcast networks and cable and satellite channels are cramming more and more onto valuable screen real estate.

Television is mimicking the personal computer, from NBC "crawls" promoting one show during another, to Bloomberg Television, a veritable patchwork quilt of business statistics and news.

"Increasingly, we're going to see TV work like computer screens," said industry analyst Larry Gerbrandt of Carmel-based Paul Kagan Associates.

"The problem with television is that it's linear, it can only do one thing at a time," he said. "This is a way of multi-tasking, and it's clear from the way people use computers and websites that they can do more than one thing at a time."

The CNN Headline News changes, part of an overhaul that includes a faster pace and new faces, is an acknowledgment that computers have affected consumer habits, said Teya Ryan, executive vice president and general manager.

With a variety of news on the screen, viewers can spot the highlights they want immediately—the kind of immediacy and choice they're used to when going online.

"People are meant to use this network, not just listen to it but use it. There's weather, sports and news when they want it," she said.

The displays are a precursor to true TV-computer interactivity in which viewers will, for instance, be able to click on a weather map icon and get their area's forecast, Ryan said.

As part of its makeover, ESPNews will roughly double the information grid at the bottom of the screen, said spokesman Mike Soltys. "Real-time" scores from games in progress also will be shown.

"Sports is a very data-intensive area and people are getting more and more information off the Internet," he said. "We want to bring that to television."

Can there be an overload? TV viewer Bruce Beasley, 44, of Corona, California, who works in the real estate industry, thinks so. "It's distracting," he said of the information already on news channels like CNN and MSNBC. His 18-year-old son, Matthew, a Web designer, disagrees.

"When I turn on ESPNews or CNN, I want news. I'd like it (an expanded display), especially if I'm trying to get a particular score or news story and don't want to wait before they rotate again. As a teenager, I'm very impatient."

He's part of the younger, computer-savvy demographic which CNN Headline News, part of the Turner Broadcasting System, expects will most easily adapt to the new format.

"Focus testing comes back off the charts," said Turner CEO Jamie Kellner. "If you get really a lot of older people, you'll start getting confusion. But with the core (audience) that you want for this, which is 18–49, 25–54, there's a very, very solid response."

ESPN also did focus-group testing and found there are limits to how much the screen can hold, spokesman Soltys said. Even the channel's planned incarnation may require an adjustment period.

"We found that while the first reaction to a screen with multiple elements was 'Boy, that's a lot of information,' sports fans learned the format and found the information they were looking for," Soltys said.

People can learn to accept data-dense television, according to UCLA psychology professor Philip J. Kellman, director of the school's cognitive science research program.

Information delivered to the eye and ear is less confusing than that coming from two visual or auditory sources, Kellman said. Consistent placement of material also helps viewers adjust. Whether that's necessarily for the better is uncertain, he said. "We seem to be trying to cram more and more information into a screen or people's lives, and even though we can learn to become better at absorbing it it's probably a bit stressful."

How the change will strike all-important advertisers is also in question. ESPNews will run its news displays during commercials while CNN Headline News is weighing such a move.

"I could make a case that it's actually good for advertisers," Gerbrandt said. "If you've got information going across the screen you're less likely to switch to another channel when the commercial comes on."

Another industry expert was skeptical. "Advertisers pay a lot of money for those commercials," said Kathy Haesele of Advanswers Media in St. Louis, a media-buying firm. "I don't know why news should be distracting the viewer."

Reprinted with permission of The Associated Press.

Review

1. The personal computer makes it possible to create lots of special text effects at little or no additional cost. With color printers, the Internet, and multimedia presentation software, words can be enlivened with colors, sizes, shapes, and even sound effects and movement. The computer screen itself—rather than paper—is often the destination point for words.
2. We're in the midst of a revolution to define how language should look. It's an exciting time in history for anyone who works with words. Text is jumping off the printed page and into cyberspace. New standards are emerging for how text should appear on-screen. And indirectly (especially with the advent of desktop publishing software), those rules are beginning to affect how text appears on paper.
3. Font choices set a mood for your words.
4. Words are an integral part of the overall design.
5. Not all computers have the same fonts, so if you create a slide show or Web page on one computer but display it on another, you might be surprised when a lot of ordinary looking default fonts pop up.
6. Bigger words tend to get noticed before smaller words. Bigger text says, "This is important, look here first." Bigger text adds emphasis or gives viewers direction in terms of where to look first.
7. If you plan to write for multimedia on a regular basis, it is a good idea to take a basic art class where you can learn about color principles and aesthetics.
8. A sound or movement can bring drama to text if properly and thoughtfully placed. Otherwise, it can just become an annoying distraction. Studies have established that the eye is drawn to motion, so use it purposefully and sparingly.
9. If emphasis techniques are overused, they can trivialize your text and the credibility of your words.
10. Colors chosen for information in your charts and graphs can actually confuse viewers if they have no apparent rhyme or reason.

Key Terms and Concepts

Costuming Visually presenting text in the most effective way.

Emphasis Using special effects to draw attention to sentences, phrases, and/or words.

Sans serif font A typeface without "tails" (*sans* is a French word meaning without).

Serif font A typeface with a finishing stroke (a little "tail" leading to the next letter).

Special effects Methods of making words stand out.

Too gray A presentation that looks too text-heavy.

Chapter Questions

1. Three things in history have largely affected the viewing and mass dissemination of words. What are they?
2. Name seven different special effects techniques for words.

Now You Try

On the CD-ROM, visit the recommended Helpful Websites for chapter 7 to find:

- An entertaining look at truly bad emphasis techniques
- Outstanding tips for creating and presenting text effectively on a Website
- Duke University tutorials on Web and interactive media design, including "Design Basic: Using Color," "The Computer Medium: Font Availability," and "Font Sizing"
- A really useful guide to fonts
- A friendly Colorwheel Fact Sheet, for nonart types
- An introductory look at color psychology
- The Website of the Color Association of the United States

Write 15 interesting facts you learned from visiting these Websites. Identify where each fact came from (by Website title and Web page address).

Unconventional Wisdom

- Older and younger viewers prefer to read larger type.
- Colors can clash with the message.

Endnotes

1. Nielsen, J. (2003, April). *Alertbox* [Online]. Retrieved from www.useit.com/alertbox/20030421.html

2. Bailey, Bob. (2002, February). More about fonts. *UI Design Update Newsletter*. Fairfield, IA: Human Factors International. Available at www.humanfactors.com/downloads/feb02.asp.

3. Color Association of the United States. www.colorassociation.com/site/join.html

Answers for Chapter 7

Chapter Questions

1. ***Three things in history have largely affected the viewing and mass dissemination of words. What are they?***

1. First, paper was perfected around A.D. 100 by the Chinese.

2. Secondly, some 1,300 years after paper made its debut, German businessman Johannes Gutenberg invented the printing press.

3. The personal computer was invented in the twentieth century.

2. ***Name seven different special effects techniques for words.***

1. <u>underlining text</u> (avoid on Websites)

2. *putting text in italics*

3. changing **a portion** of text to a different font

4. **putting text in boldface**

5. putting text in a box

6. changing the color of text

7. making text different sizes

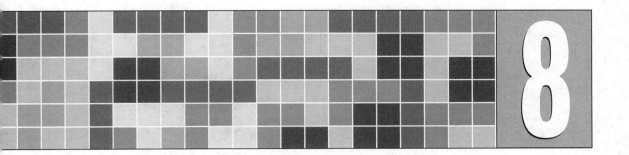

Formatting Text in a Multimedia Environment

The words of truth are simple.

—Greek tragedian Aeschylus (525–456 B.C.)[1]

OBJECTIVES

This chapter will help you learn about:

- Composition
- Contrast
- Consistency
- Spacing and layout
- Hierarchy
- A traditional format that does not work
- Some traditional formats that do work
- Words and design: working together

COMPOSITION

Artists invest time deciding how to use light, composition, and scale to guide your eyes around the canvas. Composition of elements in any work of art is carefully designed and seriously pondered. Artists and photographers strive to bring to the viewer a definite experience, feeling, or reaction. The mind's eye is instructed how to enter the work and where to proceed along the canvas or print to capture the intended message.

In the same way, your text and design need to work together to guide your viewers' eyes around your Web page or slide. In teaching how to create a slide show, I advise my students to think of each slide as its own small, independent work of art.

There is an entire field of research devoted to eye movement and how the eye operates when looking at a screen rather than paper. Research suggests that the eye focuses on small chunks of text at a time. The eye can take in one word along with four characters to the left and 15 characters to the right at any given time. This is because most of our eye receptors are clustered in the middle of the retina in a tiny area known as the fovea.

So we move our eyes when we read. And depending upon our cultural training, we prefer to read left to right or right to left. But our eye functions best when it is given a recognized system to follow.

Current eye movement research suggests that when it comes to a screen, we look at the middle first. Through the use of emphasis, our eyes must be drawn from there to wherever we are supposed to look next.

Visual elements take precedence over text. Larger chunks of text take precedence over smaller ones. Bigger letters take precedence over smaller ones. Colors take precedence over black and white. Too many factors that compete in these areas, however, result in viewer confusion.

Overuse of a particular emphasis technique can also cause confusion. WRITING TEXT IN ALL CAPITAL LETTERS, FOR EXAMPLE, CAN BECOME OVERWHELMING AND SEEM LIKE "SHOUTING" IF CARRIED TO THE EXTREME. IT CAN EASILY CREATE CONFUSION AND EVEN IRRITATION FOR VIEWERS.

Good design, combined with clear writing, presents a visual map for viewers to follow, from the most important elements to the least important ones. As a writer or editor, this means you have to organize your content succinctly and pay close attention to proper composition. What will your viewers look at first, second, and so on? Compose your content in such a way that the viewers' eyes follow a visual pattern that you have consciously developed.

Exploration

On the accompanying CD-ROM, click on the links for these two Web pages. Which one do you think has the better sense of composition? Why? Explain your point of view.

- MSN.com: www.msn.com (see Figure 8.1)
- USA Today: www.usatoday.com (see Figure 8.2)

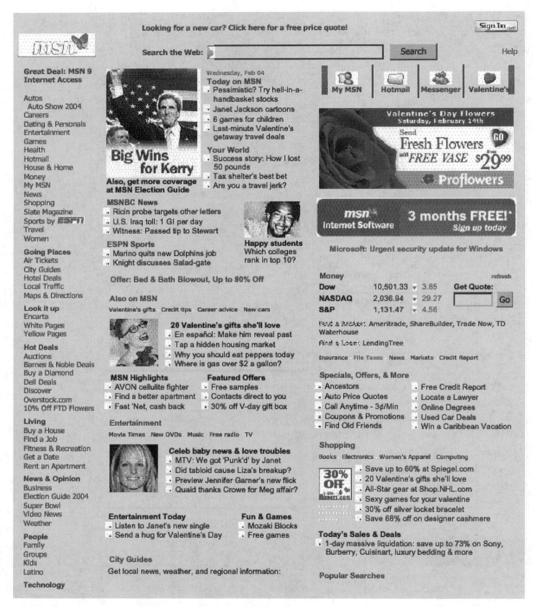

FIGURE 8.1   The MSN Website. *(Courtesy Microsoft Corporation.)*

FIGURE 8.2 The *USA Today* Website. (USA Today © *November 12, 2003. Reprinted with permission.*)

CONTRAST

"But it looked good on my computer screen." I can't count the times students have projected their PowerPoint presentations onto the projection screen only to utter these words. The biggest realization they face is that they didn't provide enough contrast between the letters of the words and the color of the background.

That light blue font may look great against the dark blue background when it's on the computer screen, but once it hits the projector screen, it can scarcely be read. Change the font color to light yellow. Exaggerate the contrast. When viewers have to try to read text projected onto a screen, the more contrast, the better. A simple rule of thumb is dark text/light background or light text/dark background.

Just because the contrast looks great on your computer screen doesn't mean it will not wash out if shown on a projector screen. So try to run your presentation ahead of time in the way you intend to show it (in a large room or small room, with lights out or lights on).

The same rule applies to a Website. It is hard enough to read small text on a computer screen, but when viewers have to try and see dark text against a dark background, they are likely to give up. It's an unnecessary burden to impose upon people who are taking the time to visit your Website.

Exploration

Which of these two slides do you think has the better contrast?

CONSISTENCY

Consistency, or continuity, helps viewers stay the course. By establishing a consistent pattern of information presentation, you ensure that viewers stay focused and understand what they are supposed to do visually and mentally. The layout of this book provides an example, with its chapter titles, headings, and subheads that have the same format from chapter to chapter. Words are also presented consistently; for example, you won't read *Web page* in one paragraph and *webpage* in another.

The process of maintaining a unified, organized look for online content is referred to as content management. Here are some ways to promote consistency:

- **Cascading style sheets:** HTML and XML coding now permit the creation of style sheets, which allow you to program and maintain consistent typographic styles and spacing from Web page to Web page. The standards you establish are automatically applied to every Website change you make, which not only improves continuity but is a big maintenance time-saver.

- **Templates:** You can create or use pre-designed type-in layouts that allow you to quickly drop new or updated content into a designated space.

   Presentation software packages offer you templates, but be careful about overusing them because audiences tend to see the same templates over and over again, which invites instant boredom. I know

I have personally endured close to a hundred slide shows featuring the Dad's Tie design template, a PowerPoint classic.

The best reasons to use templates is if you are in a hurry, if you don't know any other way to use the software, or if you are working on a team that requires different people to contribute to one presentation. Otherwise, try designing and saving your own unique templates. Just go to Format>Background and Format>Font to get started. (I teach how to do this, and it's always fun.)

Website templates are now available for content, too. If your business or news Website moves a lot of content, templates help make sure that content submitted by different people looks unified throughout your Website. A good tutorial on templates from one company, Zope, can be viewed at: www.zope.com/Demos/CentralizedSiteDesign.mov.

- **Style guides:** These are guides created by companies, universities, or individuals to make sure that spelling, grammar, punctuation, and other content considerations are handled in the same manner over and over again. (The CD-ROM that accompanies this book provides you with online style guides.) For example, you may decide the word *Website* should be one word no matter where it appears, rather than *Web site* sometimes and *Website* other times.

    Siebel eBusiness has an excellent corporate style guide that covers a multitude of topics including (but definitely not limited to):

- How to write the company's name, products, and services; for example, *e* is always italicized and lowercase (even when the *e* is at the start of a sentence or in a title)

- How to write terms common to the industry; for example, use *dot-com* rather than *dot.com*, *CD-ROM* rather than *CD-Rom*, and *double-click*, rather than *doubleclick* or *double click*

- How to write phrases common to Web usage; for example, write *Open the File menu* rather than *Drop down the File menu*

    Entire sections of the guide are devoted to avoiding slang and jargon, using bias-free language, and following basic spelling, grammar, word usage, capitalization, numerical, and punctuation rules.

    Paying this kind of attention to every detail promotes consistency—and thereby clarity—for online viewers. It also makes any Website or other multimedia presentation look crisp and professional.

When producing a slide show, you can also maintain consistency by using one main font style and a set color scheme. Again, don't overuse design templates provided by the software maker, however, or consistency can quickly turn into blandness and boredom. Try to create your own color themes and layout designs whenever possible.

SPACING AND LAYOUT

What you don't see is as important as what you do see. In design, negative space (or what is called white space in traditional printing) is an area that has no content. You can emphasize text by surrounding it with negative space. Text set apart by negative space has more presence than text that is crowded against graphics and other text. (Negative space doesn't have to be white.)

Setting your more important text in its own space surrounded by "emptiness" (negative or white space) gives it more visibility.

Exploration

On the accompanying CD-ROM, click on the links to the following Websites. Which of these two Web pages do you think makes the better use of negative space? Explain why.

- PC-Doctor: www.ws.com (see Figure 8.3)
- FedWorld: www.fedworld.gov (see Figure 8.4)

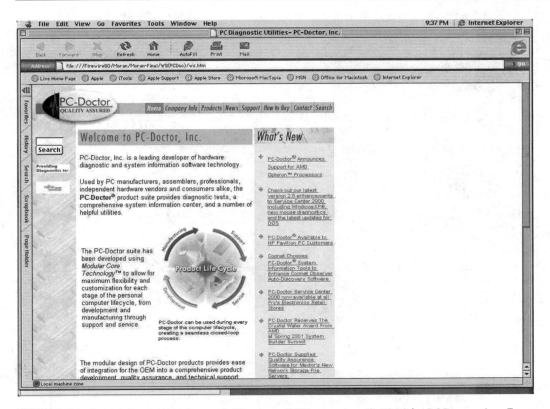

FIGURE 8.3   The PC-Doctor Web page. *(Courtesy PCDoctor, Inc. © 2003 by PCDoctor, Inc. From Website October 31, 2003.)*

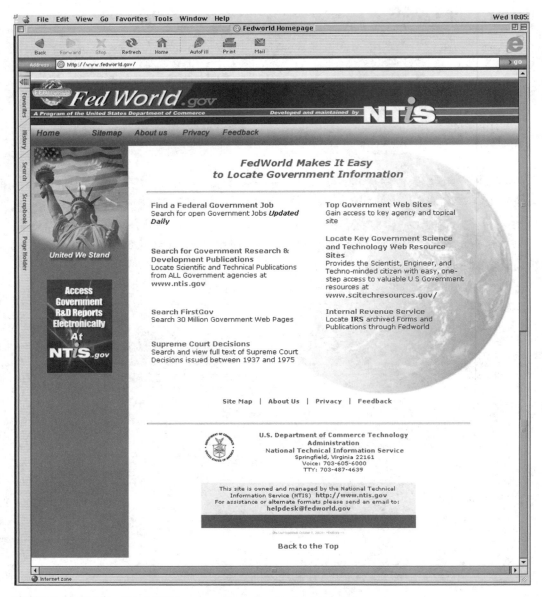

FIGURE 8.4   The FedWorld Web page. *(Courtesy Federal World.)*

Well-established theories on groupings and space have been described by the principles of perceptual organization. Also called the Gestalt Laws, they were developed by Gestalt psychologists of the 1920s and 1930s. They describe the ways that humans tend to associate certain visual placements with one another. Figure 8.5 includes examples of four of the best-known Gestalt Laws.

The moral of Gestalt Laws is that when items such as words are grouped together, they require less effort to process by the mind, which is usually a good thing. If the mind tries to group words unsuccessfully, it becomes frustrated or confused and may discard the information rather than work to process it. The mind is not a passive sponge. It actively sorts and processes input, deciding what goes together, what should be stored in memory, and what should be discarded. It selects information and imposes order.

Think, for example, of how you might view geese or pelicans flying overhead. Have you ever concluded that the birds fly in a V formation? The birds don't realize this, of course, but our human minds are programmed to think of two rows of birds converging at one end as a V shape. The birds

FIGURE 8.5   Examples of Gestalt Laws.

This is the most important thing I know.

Pass the mustard.

1. Law of proximity

Items that are placed near one another appear to be connected. Although the first sentence has absolutely nothing to do with the second sentence in the example above, the brain tries to find associated meaning between the two just because they are placed together.

This is mustard because sky is a deep blanket.

2. Law of good continuation

Items that are placed in a continuous line will tend to be grouped together. Even though the words above constitute nonsense, they are initially perceived as a sentence.

The same can be said for letters within a word. If one letter appears too far away from others in a word, it may not be perceived as part of the word; for example:

S   tudy   rather than   Study.

It is important when you present words, especially in a title, that you make sure the letters appear in proper relationship to one another. Many desktop publishing and graphic arts software programs offer kerning and leading functions for this purpose. By using these functions, you can ensure that all the letters in a word are in proper juxtaposition to one another so they are obviously part of the same word.

One mouse One mouse One mouse One mouse

Two cats Two cats Two cats Two cats

3. Law of similarity

Items that appear alike tend to be perceived as connected. So there are two word groups above rather than 16 separate disjointed words.

(continued)

FIGURE 8.5   Examples of Gestalt Laws.   *continued*

EVERYONE IS   CAPABLE
OF LEARNING

AT   ANY AGE.
                                         H
                                         O
                                         N
                                         E
                                         S
                                         T
            NO KIDDING.   YOU
                                  KNOW?

IT'S TRUE.

4. Law of common fate

Items moving in the same direction have a "common fate," making them easier to group together and, in this case, to read. Words that crisscross or adopt a seemingly random pattern are harder to comprehend and remember.

don't know their alphabet, but they understand drag and draft, which is why they fly in this "shape" we interpret as a V.

The way you arrange words on a screen will be grouped by someone's brain. If you want that person to take in your words in the manner you intend, watch carefully how you group words together. Will you wrap them around a graphic or have them stand alone? How many words do you want the viewer to consider as part of one thought?

In addition to paragraphing, you must also consider placement in multimedia. In traditional writing, words pretty much flow down a piece of paper from top to bottom, broken only by paragraphing. But in multimedia, paragraphs can sit on the left side of a screen, then on the right side of a screen, consecutively or in chunks divided by images or negative space. So be aware of the way you are arranging text. Are you grouping your content in a way that will help or hinder your viewers' comprehension level?

In terms of layout, remember that while printed documents tend to appear on paper that is taller than it is wide, multimedia presentations generally appear in spaces wider than they are tall. If you turn a piece of typing paper sideways (in landscape view), you have created the perfect planning space for Websites and slide shows.

Although monitor sizes now vary considerably, most layouts are geared toward 640 × 480 pixels (a widely accepted estimate of screen size). So when considering layout designs for your Website or slide presentation, think sideways.

HIERARCHY

In companies and kingdoms, there are hierarchies—structures of organization leading from top to bottom. Multimedia presentations need hierarchies, too, so that the viewer doesn't sense chaos when looking at a slide or Web page.

Printed newspapers have perhaps the best-known word hierarchies. Look at the front page of any newspaper. Which story does the paper consider the main, or most important, story of the day? It is the story with the biggest headline or the one running across the topmost part of the page. Stories of secondary importance run toward the middle of the page with somewhat smaller headlines, and so on down the page. (Visit the Newseum at www.newseum.org/todaysfrontpages to see an instant selection of many of the day's front pages from around the world.)

Here are the elements that help establish hierarchy:

- **Size of type:** Bigger words carry more weight than smaller words. A word set in 36-point type will have more presence on-screen than a word set in 24-point type. That's why the use of headlines has always been a way to build hierarchy.

- **Emphasis techniques:** Words that have been given special emphasis because they look different than other words carry more weight than words with no special emphasis. They become more important because they are noticed first.

- **Page placement:** Where words are situated on a Web page or slide gives them a certain weight and importance. Words placed toward the top tend to be read first.

- **Independence:** Words that stand alone on a page surrounded by white space (or negative space) tend to have more importance to the eye than words crowded together in a paragraph or chunk.

Exploration

On the accompanying CD-ROM, click on the following links and compare these two home pages. One has a clear hierarchy, and the other doesn't. Which is which? What could be done to improve the home page with the poorer hierarchy? Explain your answer.

- Refdesk.com: www.refdesk.com (see Figure 8.6)
- Librarians' Index to the Internet: lii.org (see Figure 8.7)

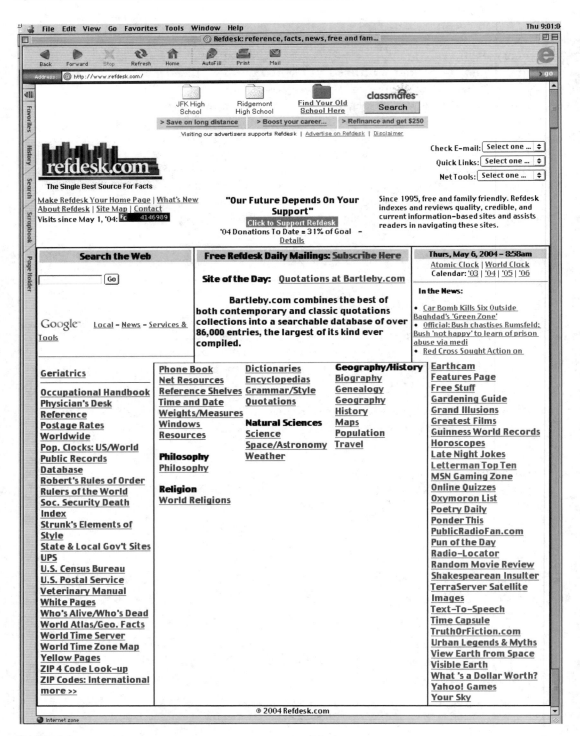

FIGURE 8.6   The refdesk.com home page. *(Courtesy refdesk.com.)*

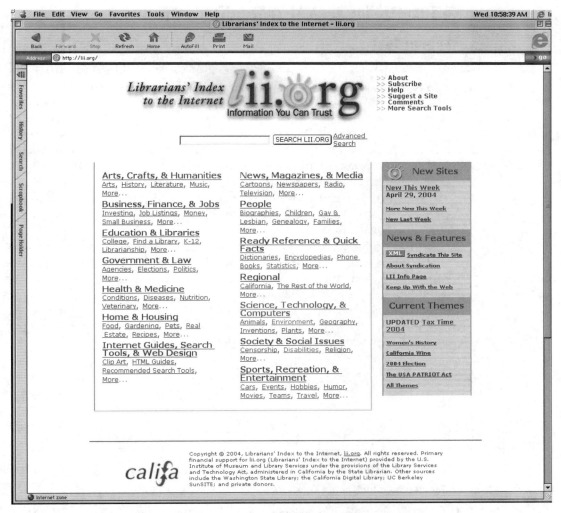

FIGURE 8.7 The Librarians' Index to the Internet home page. *(Reprinted with permission of Librarian's Index to the Internet.)*

A TRADITIONAL FORMAT THAT DOESN'T WORK

Lots of Text

When we write for print, we may go on for pages and pages. But this kind of writing on-screen—particularly as it relates to the Web—requires viewers to use a scroll bar. Having to negotiate a scroll bar and read at the same time is disconcerting.

So as much as possible, try to avoid text that runs so long that viewers have to scroll. And scrolling from side to side is a definite no-no because it completely interferes with a viewer's train of thought. It is equivalent to setting document margins that are wider than the paper.

The current trend in home page design is not to have any scrolling at all. Good writing and good design easily get visitors from the front page to where they want to go.

If you do have a long document that might equate to a page in a book, try to divide it up with boxes that contain break-out quotes. Better yet, provide your viewers with a well-written summary on the Web page and the full document as a PDF they can download and print out for easier handheld reading. Not every document has to be fully displayed on a Website. PDF versions allow viewers to print out or download to their own computers what they want to read in more detail.

Exploration

On the accompanying CD-ROM, click on the links to the following Websites. Which home page does a better job avoiding a text-heavy effect?

- MEDLINEplus: www.nlm.nih.gov/medlineplus (see Figure 8.8)
- MedExplorer: www.medexplorer.com (see Figure 8.9)

FIGURE 8.8 The MEDLINEplus home page. *(Courtesy MedlinePlus Health Information.)*

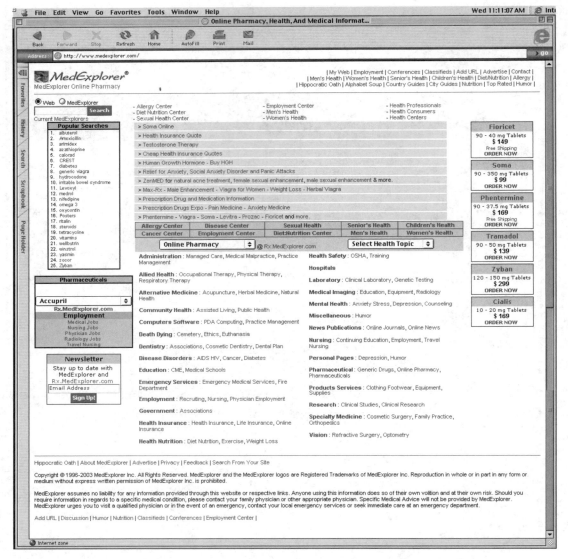

FIGURE 8.9 The MedExplorer home page. *(Courtesy MedExplorer Online® Pharmacy.)*

FIGURE 8.10   A wordy multimedia text box.

In a multimedia presentation, it is possible to have too many words when you don't have that many words at all! Look at the example in Figure 8.10, noting the text bubble. It purports to teach salespeople how to be polite to customers.

Many times, online training sites employ text bubbles for presenting quizzes and other training materials. But even in these cases, careful attention must be paid to just how much text gets piled into a text box. The example in Figure 8.10 contains 65 words, far too many for a text bubble. Besides, how many people really talk in this stilted and corporate-sounding manner? The text is artificial and print-oriented.

Exploration

Rewrite the text bubble in Figure 8.10 so that it is shorter and sounds more real. Try to reduce the number of words by at least half. After you come up with your own, see one suggested answer on page 179.

Filling a Web page with lots of words results in a cluttered look. Not everything you have to say needs to fit on one page, especially your home page. That's the beauty of the Web—you can make more pages! With good organization, your home page can be the top level that carefully guides users down into each sublevel of your site.

Exploration

In an effort to look like "real" newspapers, online versions may use small type and long columns of text. They may make limited use of negative space and hierarchy. The homepages may require a lot of scrolling. Take a look at the three examples listed below. Do these sites make the best use of multimedia-style writing and display? Why or why not? Explain your answers.

- Seattle Times (see Figure 8.11)
  http://seattletimes.nwsource.com/html/home/
- Wall Street Journal online (see Figure 8.12)
  http://online.wsj.com/public/us
- Herald Sun (see Figure 8.13)
  http://www.heraldsun.news.com.au/

Text Plus

I'm old enough to remember newsroom "rewrite desks." Today, it might be advisable for print-based newspapers going online to develop rewrite desks so that print-based copy can be restructured for more appropriate presentation on the Web.

This, of course, would require newspapers and other print-based publications to have multimedia writers who understand both the demands of print-style writing and multimedia writing. Simply taking stories prepared for print editions and sticking them online does a disservice to online viewers. It also diminishes the value of the print version of the paper.

Interestingly, one online newspaper that makes a commendable effort to use multimedia design and writing effectively is USAToday.com.

FIGURE 8.11 The *Seattle Times* Website. *(Courtesy of* The Seattle Times.*)*

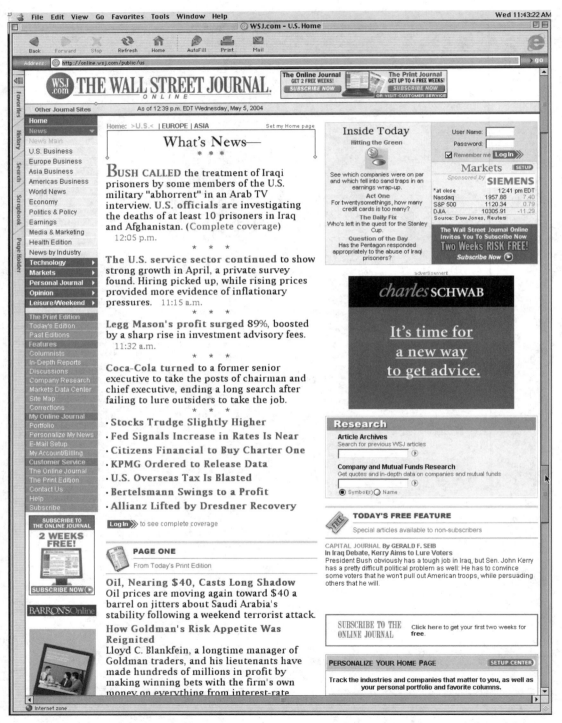

FIGURE 8.12 *The Wall Street Journal* Website. (*Reprinted with permission of* The Wall Street Journal, Copyright ©2003 Dow Jones & Company. All rights reserved.)

FIGURE 8.13 The *Herald Sun* Website. *(Courtesy of* The Herald & Weekly Times Ltd.*)*

When the print version of *USA Today* first arrived on the scene, traditional print-oriented news experts were quick to criticize its approach as flashy and superficial. The newspaper encouraged its writers to create crisp, succinct stories that did not require page jumps (having to go inside the paper to read the rest of the stories). It used color, dramatic hierarchy, generous negative spacing, and other techniques that just didn't seem traditionally print-oriented.

Now it seems, as far as multimedia writing and display are concerned, *USA Today* was ahead of its time.

Newspapers should encourage people to subscribe to the print version for longer, more in-depth analysis of news and issues. Clear, bright, concise overviews are more appropriate for the online versions. Give viewers the chance to download the print versions (or subscribe to the paper) if they want to read that six-part series on the history of the electoral college system and how it continues to impact presidential elections today.

The moral is that online and print versions of newspapers can complement one another. One is not better than the other. They serve different purposes and often different audiences.

It behooves newspaper publishers to have a clear understanding of the purpose of each. Print versions serve mostly local populations. Online versions serve the world. Many times in my communications courses I introduce exchange and foreign students to their online newspapers back home. They are amazed, happy, and comforted to find online versions of newspapers they read in print back in their home villages and towns. It gives them a sense of still being connected to fellow citizens overseas and over national borders.

When I teach the Internet to retirement-aged users, I encourage them to check out online versions of newspapers if they are contemplating retiring to another town or state. Before I know it, they are also visiting the websites of newspapers in the towns where their grown children live.

The online revolution seems to have caught many traditional, print-oriented publications off-guard. For some the initial tendency was to dismiss the importance of Web editions outright. Quickly, though, most moved to creating "print versions" online. Now at last many news organizations are beginning the important task of really assessing how printed newspapers, journals, and magazines can complement and be complemented by their online versions.

How should they be alike? What are their distinctive differences based on the fact that one version appears on paper and the other version appears on a computer screen? How should the writing and display be modified from traditional to multimedia settings?

It is exciting that these discussions have begun in earnest.

SOME TRADITIONAL FORMATS THAT DO WORK

Paragraphing or "Chunking"

As mentioned above, we are physiologically and culturally trained to absorb chunks of text in organized ways. One of those Western conventions is paragraphing. If you are writing a traditional business letter, you may choose to indent paragraphs or to block them with a space between each paragraph. Both styles are acceptable, as long as your choice remains consistent within any one document.

Here are examples of the same passage in both indented and blocked paragraph style.

INDENTED STYLE

One of the most important aspects of deciding whether or not to get a dog is your lifestyle. Are you an active, outdoorsy person? Or do you enjoy reading books by the fireplace? Dogs have various sizes and temperaments to complement your way of life.

Another thing to consider is your personality type. Are you outgoing and happy-go-lucky—a party animal? Or do you prefer a more solitary, introspective environment?Some breeds of dog are very social, while others prefer to bond with one person and live a more self-contained existence.

BLOCK STYLE

One of the most important aspects of deciding whether or not to get a dog is your lifestyle. Are you an active, outdoorsy person? Or do you enjoy reading books by the fireplace? Dogs have various sizes and temperaments to complement your way of life.

Another thing to consider is your personality type. Are you outgoing and happy-go-lucky—a party animal? Or do you prefer a more solitary, introspective environment? Some breeds of dog are very social, while others prefer to bond with one person and live a more self-contained existence.

My preference is to use block style if I don't have a lot of text to place, and indented style for longer written pieces. Block style requires more space but is easier for the eye to "chunk" than the indented style.

The Web affords the opportunity to really use chunking. You can write a headline and a one-line description, then use the headline as a link to a separate page where the entire article runs.

Here is an example from the online edition of ENN, the Environmental News Network at enn.com:

Responsible Investing *more . . .*

How can green habits grow your investment portfolio? Check out the Socially Responsible Investing topics page to find out. *more . . .*

By clicking the headline or the word *more*, users leave the home page to read the full story.

Or consider this example from the home page of National Geographic News at news.nationalgeographic.com:

Rain Forest Plan Blends Drug Research, Conservation

Together with Panamanian researchers, a pair of American biologists have proposed a plan they say will be more effective to identify medical cures found in tropical rain forest plants and animals. GO>>

Click the headline or the word GO to get to the Web page containing this story.

Here's a final example from the home page of Science Daily at www.sciencedaily.com:

Northwest Salmon Could Face Same Fate As Those In Northeast, England

New laws protected salmon spawning grounds in 17 rivers, prohibiting the streams from being blocked with dams or fishing nets and . . . >full story

In this case, users click the headline or the words *full story* to visit the internal Web page containing the rest of the article.

When creating this kind of link, you may want to have the story open in a separate window hanging partially over the home page. When users finish reading the story, they can click the window closed and automatically be back on the home page, where they can easily find other stories to click.

Inverted Pyramid Style

One of the most revered conventions for presenting newspaper text is called the inverted pyramid style. Taught for years in journalism schools, it is based on the need to put the most important information first and the least important information last.

Picture an upside-down triangle like this:

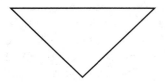

The most important facts and information fill the top level. The least important, peripheral information winds up at the bottom. That's why writing a good "lead paragraph" (or first paragraph) is very important in journalism. And reporters don't usually spend a lot of time writing a big, dramatic ending because it is liable to get cut anyway to make way for advertising.

This formatting technique stemmed from the habit of chopping off stories at the bottom to create space for print ads right before deadline. Especially when writing for a Website, your content may not get chopped off at the bottom for ad placement, but the reality is that viewers may not hang in there long enough to read every word (especially if you make them scroll a lot). When people visit your Website, your home page should give them the most important information about your site and its mission.

As they click deeper into your site, they can get secondary, then tertiary information. They may "chop off" your ending by clicking to another site altogether before they drop down to your fourth or fifth level.

Similarly, with slide presentations, your audience may be thinking about lunch by the time you get to the final slide. So try putting the most important information as close to the beginning of the presentation as possible. Leave the last slides for a wrap-up or review of key points, and for a list of resources. Save that exciting ending for your novel.

Exploration

Visit Microsoft's press release section at www.microsoft.com/presspass.

Then visit Apple's press release section at www.apple.com/pr.

Look at several press releases on each site. Which Website has press releases suited for multimedia, and which one seems more traditionally print oriented?

Now pretend that your boss at 1SunPower, Inc., has asked you to organize the facts listed below for an online press release to be posted on 1SunPower's Website. Number the list of 10 facts from 1 (for most important) to 10 (for least important). Then write a press release based on the order in which you numbered each item, putting the most important fact first and the least important fact last.

Add a catchy title to the top of your press release. Use chunking and other techniques.

After you have finished, turn to page 180 to find suggested answers and a completed press release based on this information. See how yours compares.

Fact Sheet

_____ Your company: 1SunPower, Inc. (a company that provides power using the sun as a solar energy source)

_____ Address of 1SunPower, Inc.: 102 Sunshine Way, San Francisco, CA 94001; (415) 555–2323; www.1sunpower.com

_____ Event being announced: 1SunPower has installed a large photovoltaic solar-powered energy system at the Grapevine Winery. The Grapevine Winery is one of the largest wineries in America. Using sun power instead of expensive electric energy, the

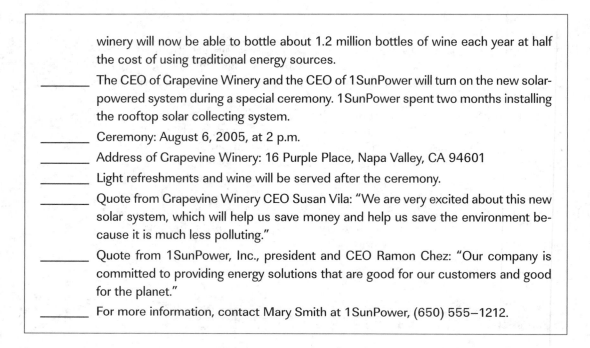

winery will now be able to bottle about 1.2 million bottles of wine each year at half the cost of using traditional energy sources.

_____ The CEO of Grapevine Winery and the CEO of 1SunPower will turn on the new solar-powered system during a special ceremony. 1SunPower spent two months installing the rooftop solar collecting system.

_____ Ceremony: August 6, 2005, at 2 p.m.

_____ Address of Grapevine Winery: 16 Purple Place, Napa Valley, CA 94601

_____ Light refreshments and wine will be served after the ceremony.

_____ Quote from Grapevine Winery CEO Susan Vila: "We are very excited about this new solar system, which will help us save money and help us save the environment because it is much less polluting."

_____ Quote from 1SunPower, Inc., president and CEO Ramon Chez: "Our company is committed to providing energy solutions that are good for our customers and good for the planet."

_____ For more information, contact Mary Smith at 1SunPower, (650) 555–1212.

WORDS AND DESIGN: WORKING TOGETHER

If a Website does nothing but display print-style text on a screen, it really isn't achieving its true potential. A scientist may write a paper describing cell division, but the Web is capable of showing it through both words and animation. An animation illustrating cell division will be greatly complemented by well-written text explaining the process in clear, complete, accurate, objective, and concise terms.

On the other hand, if a Website is loaded with graphics, the question is why? At least for now, it takes more time to load Websites with lots of animations and graphics, when well-chosen words might suffice just as well. Carefully weigh what every graphic adds to comprehension before substituting an image for text. Download times aside, a multimedia production that is overloaded with graphics can easily become cluttered and hard to comprehend. William B. Sanders describes one poorly designed site: "The content is smothered in a train wreck of techno-pieces happily added by the Web page designer. It is reminiscent of the early days of desktop publishing. The desktop publisher, in a rush to use all of her new fonts, ended up with a page that looked like a ransom note. A clear page does a better job."[2]

When words and design work together in a unified presentation, viewers are treated to an efficient, stress-free, positive enrichment experience. They plan that trip to Ireland, or find out how much that car will cost them, or buy that book, or learn to speak Spanish, or ponder the news of the day, or accomplish any number of things.

People can learn things by reading them in a book, but the great gift of multimedia is that it allows people to learn by reading *and* experiencing events, activities, processes, or interactions. If we read about something and have a significant experience related to what we read, it can enhance our memory and learning. It can reinforce a concept or idea in a much more significant and lasting way than just reading a passage of text.

Some of the unique tools that multimedia permits us to use to build that transforming, interactive experience for viewers include:

1. **Tutorials:** Writing and design can work together to guide a viewer through a learning experience step by step.
2. **Games:** Children learn by playing, and so can adults if words and design create a fun environment.
3. **Monitored chats:** On the Web, viewers can visit firsthand with experts and celebrities.
4. **Group discussions:** Online message boards and discussions provide opportunities for interchange and growth.
5. **Virtual field trips:** These take viewers to locations for firsthand observation.
6. **Demos:** A well-designed, well-written demonstration with high-quality images allows viewers to see up-close how to do something new.
7. **Quizzes:** These allow viewers to review what they have absorbed before taking in new information.

A multimedia communications specialist has a working knowledge of the technology and design requirements of these tools, as well as a strong sense of how to write explanatory text for them without lapsing into dry technical-style writing.

Exploration

Go on the Internet and find good examples of *three* of the interactive tools listed above. Explain why you like them, paying close attention to how words are used effectively in each of your three examples.

See page 181 for some other examples. (They are also on the CD-ROM.)

In summary, there are entire courses offered on graphic design, but our interest here is to present text as an integrated part of an overall design. With that in mind, here are some final concepts to keep in mind:

1. *The eye is drawn to change.* If you suddenly change the color or emphasis of your text, or give it movement, the viewer's eye will go there first. If the movement is persistent enough, the viewer's eye will return to it and lose sight of whatever else you intended to impart on the screen. If your Website has the word *Sale!* flashing repeatedly on-screen, will it cause your viewer to lose concentration in relation to the rest of your content? Consider how long you want something to stand out before you tone it down to give viewers a chance to look at the rest of your page or slide.

2. *Attention is drawn to the unusual.* Put four apples and one orange on a table and the eye will gravitate toward the orange. It is the unusual item in the bunch. Ironically, this is one reason the eye is drawn to misspellings on-screen. A misspelled word is unusual in comparison to all the words spelled correctly. Many times I have been witness to the impact of a misspelled word in the middle of a presentation. I can hear the whispering begin as audience members check with one another to see who has noticed the misspelling on a slide. The mistake becomes the object of attention.

3. *Subtlety can be powerful.* An understated approach works because people are so used to presentations that "scream" at them. One well-known footwear company uses a plain dark background and white letters that read, "Just do it." Its logo is a simple check mark. In comparison to all the flashy, intense, loud, and colorful advertising competition out there, this slogan is memorable because of its simplicity. Some politicians employ this technique by standing in front of backgrounds with slogans or logos they want people to remember. And in the movies, the practice of product placement is another subtle way advertisers try to get you to think about their products without aiming a blaring ad directly at you.

Exploration

On the accompanying CD-ROM, click on links for the following two Websites.

Which home page do you think incorporates words, graphics, and design elements more effectively? Could anything be improved even more?

- Discovery Telescopes: www.discovery-telescopes.com (see Figure 8.15)
- Meade Telescopes: www.meade.com (see Figure 8.16)

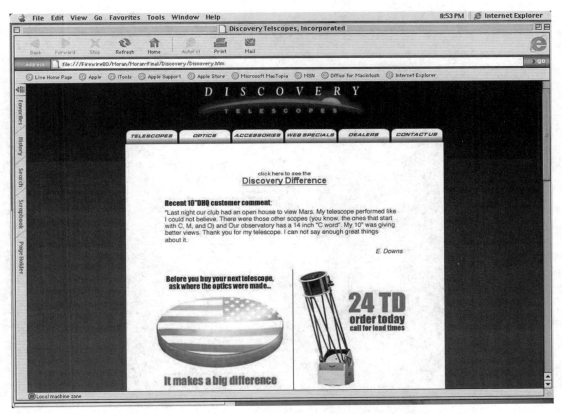

FIGURE 8.15   The Discovery Telescopes home page. *(Reprinted with permission of Discovery Telescopes.)*

FIGURE 8.16   The Meade home page. *(Courtesy Meade Instruments Corporation.)*

Review

1. Your text and design need to work together to guide your viewers' eyes.
2. Our eyes function best when given a recognized system to follow.
3. Visual elements take precedence over text.
4. Larger chunks of text take precedence over smaller ones.
5. Bigger letters take precedence over smaller ones.
6. Colors take precedence over black and white.
7. Too many factors that compete in these areas result in viewer confusion.
8. Overuse of a particular emphasis technique can also cause confusion.
9. Good design, combined with clear writing, presents a visual map for viewers to follow from the most important elements to the least important ones.
10. The more contrast, the better when viewers have to read text projected onto a screen.
11. A simple rule of thumb is dark text/light background or light text/dark background.
12. Consistency, or continuity, helps viewers stay the course.
13. You can emphasize text by surrounding it with negative space.
14. Well-established theories on groupings and space are described by the principles of perceptual organization.
15. If the mind tries to group words unsuccessfully, it becomes frustrated or confused and may discard the information rather than work to process it.
16. While printed documents tend to appear on paper that is taller than it is wide, multimedia presentations generally appear in spaces wider than they are tall.
17. Multimedia presentations need hierarchies so that the viewer doesn't sense chaos when viewing a slide or Web page.
18. Not every document has to be fully displayed on a Website. PDF versions allow viewers to print out what they want to read in more detail or download to their own computers.
19. Multimedia allows people to learn by reading *and* experiencing events, activities, processes, or interactions.
20. The eye is drawn to change.
21. Attention is drawn to the unusual.
22. Subtlety can be powerful.

Key Terms and Concepts

Inverted pyramid style   A journalism convention for organizing content from the most to the least important information.

Negative space   Also called white space, it is an area that is intentionally devoid of content or images.

Chapter Questions

1. What are three ways to promote consistency?
2. What four things help establish hierarchy for words?
3. What two different styles are used to create paragraphs?
4. What are seven ways to build an interactive experience for viewers?

Now You Try

Part A

On the CD-ROM, visit the recommended Helpful Websites for chapter 8 to find:

- Duke University's Center for Instructional Technology tutorial on "Using White Space"
- The Yale Web Style Guide
- A well-written and well-presented look at formatting and other issues
- One consultant's views on new media design, especially related to newspapers
- A helpful presentation about how preparing Web text differs from other types of editing and formatting
- A look at how parallelism may improve readability
- An introduction to content management

Write 15 interesting facts you learned from visiting these Websites. Identify where each fact came from (by Website title and Web page address).

Part B

On the CD-ROM, open the "Crafting Multimedia Text" folder, and click "Explore the Basics." Complete this section.

Unconventional Wisdom

- Chunking text (using bullets, spaces, numbered lists, informal tables, logic trees) makes it easier to read.
- Flushed left text is easier to read than centered or flushed right text.

Endnotes

1. *The Columbia world of quotations.* (1996). New York: Columbia University Press.
2. Sanders, W. B. (2000). Creating learning-centered courses for the World Wide Web. Boston: Allyn & Bacon.

Answers for Chapter 8

Here is one possible revision for the text bubble in Figure 8.10 on page 163.

Exploration

Below are answers to the exercise on page 171.

__10__	Your company: 1SunPower, Inc. (a company that provides power using the sun as a solar energy source)
__9__	Address of 1SunPower, Inc.
__1__	Event being announced
__2__	The CEO of Grapevine Winery and the CEO of 1SunPower will turn on the new solar-powered system during a special ceremony. 1SunPower spent two months installing the rooftop solar collecting system.
__5__	Ceremony: August 6, 2005, at 2 p.m.
__6__	Address of Grapevine Winery
__8__	Light refreshments and wine will be served after the ceremony.
__3__	Quote from Grapevine Winery CEO Susan Vila
__4__	Quote from 1SunPower, Inc., president and CEO Ramon Chez
__7__	For more information, contact Mary Smith.

Here is a sample press release based on the facts and the order from the fact sheet.

Grapevine Makes Wine from Sunshine

One of the largest wineries in the United States will now run on sun power. 1SunPower has installed a large photovoltaic solar-powered energy system at the Grapevine Winery.

Using sun power instead of expensive electric energy, the winery will now be able to bottle about 1.2 million bottles of wine each year at half the cost of using traditional energy sources.

The CEO of Grapevine Winery and the CEO of 1SunPower will turn on the new solar-powered system during a special ceremony. 1SunPower spent two months installing the rooftop solar collecting system.

"We are very excited about this new solar system, which will help us save money and help us save the environment because it is much less polluting," said Grapevine Winery CEO Susan Vila.

"Our company is committed to providing energy solutions that are good for our customers and good for the planet," 1SunPower, Inc., president and CEO Ramon Chez explained.

Ceremony: August 6, 2005, at 2 p.m.

Address: Grapevine Winery, 16 Purple Place, Napa Valley, CA 94601

For more information, contact Mary Smith at 1SunPower, (650) 555–1212.

Light refreshments and wine will be served after the ceremony.
1SunPower, Inc., 102 Sunshine Way, San Francisco, CA 94001, (415)
555–2323; www.1sunpower.com (Providing power using the sun as a solar
energy source)

Exploration

Here are some Websites that represent possible answers to the exercise on
page 173.

Tutorials: iMovie, etc.sccoe.k12.ca.us/i2000/00mod/1_mm/imov.
html; MS PowerPoint, www.electricteacher.com/tutorial3.htm

Games: FunBrain, www.funbrain.com; Build-A-Prairie,
www.bellmuseum.org/mnideals/prairie/build/index.html

Monitored chats: Space and Astronomy, space.about.com/
mpchat.htm; Art and Technology, arttech.about.com/mpchat.htm

Group discussions: WebMD Health, boards.webmd.com/
roundtable.asp;
Pets.ca Bulletin Board, www.pets.ca/forum/index.php

Virtual field trips: Virtual Cave,
www.goodearthgraphics.com/virtcave.html; Half Hollow Hills
Central School District Virtual Tour,
www.halfhollowhills.k12.ny.us/hhhtemp/tour.html

Demos: ExperForms/Adobe PDF Demo, adobe.webbase.com; Havok
Xtra Game Demos, oldsite.havok.com/xtra/xdev/demospage.html

Quizzes: ColorQuiz, www.colorquiz.com; Kingdomality,
www.kingdomality.com

Chapter Questions

1. *What are three ways to promote consistency?*

1. Cascading style sheets: HTML and XML coding now allow for the
   creation of style sheets, which allow you to program and maintain
   consistent typographic styles and spacing from Web page to Web
   page.

2. Templates: You can create or use pre-designed type-in layouts that
   allow you to quickly drop new or updated content into a designated
   space. Presentation software packages offer templates. And Website
   templates are now available for content, too. If your business or news
   Website moves a lot of content, templates help make sure that
   everything everyone is submitting looks unified throughout your
   Website.

3. Style guides: These are guides created by companies, universities, or
   individuals to make sure that spelling, grammar, punctuation, and

other content considerations are handled in the same manner over and over again.

2. ***What four things help establish hierarchy for words?***

1. Size of type: Bigger words carry more weight than smaller words. A word set in 36-point type will have more presence on-screen than a word set in 24-point type. That's why the use of headlines has always been a way to build hierarchy.

2. Emphasis techniques: Words that have been given special emphasis because they look different than other words carry more weight than words with no special emphasis. They are noticed first.

3. Page placement: Where words are situated on a Web page or slide gives them a certain weight and importance. Words placed toward the top tend to be read first.

4. Independence: Words that stand alone on a page surrounded by white space (or negative space) tend to have more importance to the eye than words crowded together in a paragraph or chunk.

3. ***What two different styles are used to create paragraphs?***

Block style and indented style

4. ***What are seven ways to build an interactive experience for viewers?***

1. Tutorials: Writing and design can work together to guide a viewer through a learning experience step by step.

2. Games: Children learn by playing, and so can adults if words and design create a fun environment.

3. Monitored chats: On the Web, viewers can visit firsthand with experts and celebrities.

4. Group discussions: Online message boards and discussions provide opportunities for interchange and growth.

5. Virtual field trips: These take viewers to locations for firsthand observation.

6. Demos: A well-designed, well-written demonstration with high-quality images allows viewers to see up-close how to do something new.

7. Quizzes: These allow viewers to review what they have absorbed before taking in new information.

9

Special Considerations for Websites

When words reach the tip of your tongue, hold back half of them.

—Chinese proverb[1]

OBJECTIVES

This chapter will help you learn:

- The organizational questions to answer
- Construction basics for the Web
- Why interactivity is the heart of the Internet
- How educational theory applies to your viewers
- How to utilize hyperlinks

What is most striking about words on the Web is their ability to travel. An online acquaintance of mine posted a comment to other members of an online discussion group. His intention was to share an insight with his peers. One of those who read the comment copied and pasted it into an e-mail to another friend. It was forwarded to others and wound up appearing on various Websites. It was then added to the *Columbia World of Quotations*, a respected source of outstanding and memorable quotes. Now it has been used in books (including mine—see p. 75!), theses, course syllabi, numerous Websites, and probably many other places.

The point is, that whatever words you put online can travel quickly and live long, courtesy of copy and paste functions, e-mail, discussion groups, online quotation collections, and groups of authors, educators, journalists, and students. Remember that whenever you post on the Web, whether on a Website, a discussion group, or as an e-mail or instant message, if you write something brilliant, it may travel the cyber highway forever. If you write something ridiculous, wrong, or stupid, it may travel the cyber highway forever, too. Either way, odds are your name (and possibly your reputation) will stay attached to it.

THE ORGANIZATIONAL ESSENTIALS TO CONSIDER

A Website is the "electronic book" you never quit writing. Just like with any book, proper organization helps with orientation. On a home page, the Four Essentials particularly help viewers. Let's review them:

1. Title. This is the name of your Website.

Exploration

Here are five imaginary Website titles for a Website concerned with discount Hawaiian vacation packages. Which title do you think most clearly describes the purpose of the Website?

Aloha
Hawaiian Vacation Deals!
Travel to Hawaii!
Get Away Today
Island Adventures

2. Table of contents, or navigation bar. In a book, you look for the table of contents to find out how the book "works." On a Website, the navigation bar serves the same function. It shows people what each chapter (or Web page) covers. And they can click directly from the navigation bar to the "chapter" they want to see. The navigation bar requires the right words. The words may serve as the links or they may appear on "buttons," but they must be short and to the point. It helps if they suggest action, such as *Find Bargains* vs. *Bargains* or *Grab Latest Headlines* vs. *Headlines*. The navigation bar needs to be visible no matter what page visitors are on within your Website. It needs to be in a prominent place so viewers never feel lost on your site. If the words on the navigation bar do not quickly and clearly describe what will be found on a specific Web page, viewers may choose not to bother finding out because it takes extra time to click to the "mystery page" and click back. Do not change the words on the navigation bar from Web page to Web page. If your Home button (the one that returns you to the home page) says *Home* on one page, it should not say, *Go back to home page* on another Web page. Be consistent on all pages.

Exploration

Go on the Internet and find the navigation bar (which may consist of "buttons" or words) for three different Websites. Which navigation bars do you think feature clear, crisp directional writing? Which could use improvement? What words would you substitute? Present your findings.

3. Blurb. This silly-sounding word is a magazine-based tradition that applies well to any Website. Somewhere high on the first page of your Website (your home page), there needs to be a statement of the site's purpose. This statement may consist of one sentence, one short paragraph, or even a few words. But it must be visible within a few seconds of a viewer's arrival, and it must explain the site's purpose. No matter how well known a company or other entity thinks it is, its Website must still have a blurb. A journalism axiom is "Never assume," and this definitely applies to Websites with worldwide audiences.

Here are actual blurbs taken from Websites in October 2003:

- **SpectraCom** (www.spectracom.com) has two blurbs on its home page: a short introductory blurb, "Your global guide to interactive strategies," and a bit lower on the page, a longer explanatory blurb, "SpectraCom provides clients with global interactive strategies, Internet services, e-commerce and web development, online marketing, and strategic planning and research."

- The blurb for the **U. S. Geological Survey** (www.usgs.gov) reads, "Federal source for science about the Earth, its natural and living resources, natural hazards, and the environment. More about USGS . . . "

- The introductory blurb for **Wells Fargo** (www.wellsfargo.com) simply says, "View Your Accounts" and "Online Banking & Brokerage." Its second, longer, explanatory blurb says, "Set up your accounts online" and "View your accounts online in less than a minute. Get Started Now."

- The blurb for **Special Species Project** (www.specialspecies.com) reads, "Welcome to the project-based learning adventure! See what happens when teachers, classroom advisors, and K-12 students explore plants, animals and habitats together."

- The blurb for **Operation TeddyCare** (teddycare.coastside.net) reads, "Helping kids bear adversity . . . Please send us new Teddy Bears for kids worldwide! This grassroots effort works because YOU care."

Exploration

Visit five Websites. Find their blurbs, and write them down. Could you improve them or do you think they are clear, concise, and complete?

4. Introduction or lead-in. This tells viewers where to start. It may accompany a large image or stand alone, but somewhere near the top of the page viewers need one set of words that is dominant to help them get oriented. Like the main headline on the front of a newspaper, this lead head-

line serves as the official starting point for the eye. It urges the users to enter the Website, and it must be frequently updated.

Looking at the October 2003, Wells Fargo home page again, here is its
lead headline, located near the top of the page:

> Email Hoax: Protect yourself from an <u>email hoax</u> that is making its way
> across the Internet.

The words <u>email hoax</u> link users to a timely article that will not stay on
the Website for any great length of time. But the article serves to entice new
and repeat visitors deeper into the Website. The lead headline, with ever-
changing, frequently updated content, keeps the Website looking "fresh."

Many home pages also have **regular features** or **sub-navigation bars**.
On the Wells Fargo home page, for example, are these regular features (un-
derlines are links):

Check Today's Rates

<u>Home Mortgage,</u> <u>Home Equity,</u> and <u>more.</u>

Learn About

<u>Credit Planning,</u> <u>Retirement,</u> and <u>more.</u>

These features remain the same on the home page and serve to link
users to standing pages within the Website.

On the Wells Fargo home page, the main navigation buttons are: *Individuals, Small Business, Commercial,* and *About Wells Fargo.* Each of these buttons links to a sub-navigation bar of more choices. When you click
Individuals, for example, it brings up a sub-navigation bar from which you
can make other choices. The sub-navigation bar reads:

Banking

Online Banking

Bill Pay

Checking & Savings

ATM & Check Card

Time Accounts (CDs)

More >>

Loans & Credit

Credit Cards

Home Equity Loans

Home Mortgage

Student Loans

Auto Loans

More >>

Investing & Insurance

Brokerage

IRAs

Mutual Funds

Financial Consultants

Insurance

More >>

So it is possible to have top-level navigation bars that lead to sublevel navigation bars. This setup is generally reserved for more complex Websites.

At this point in the book, you should be able to formulate a planning document that will keep you on track as you build your Website. If you can't address certain areas, go back in the book and review the relevant topic.

Exploration

To make sure you have fully planned your Website, consider the following:

1. Title of Website and blurb (For review, see chapter 4.)
2. Audience for Website (For review, see chapters 2, 6, and 9.)
   - Who are they demographically?
   - What is their baseline knowledge level? (For review, see chapter 4.)
3. New information you will impart through your Website (For review, see chapter 4.) What will visitors learn that they may not know now?
4. Goal of the Website (For review, see chapter 2.)
5. Objective of the Website (For review, see chapter 2.)
6. List of quotes, images, or links to any other Websites that will be used on this Website (For review, see chapter 4.)
7. List of tools for interactivity and/or feedback that will be used on this Website (Read on in this chapter.)
8. List of any jargon, acronyms, or terminology that need defining (For review, see chapter 5.)
9. Mission statement (See next "Exploration" box.)

Exploration

Write a mission statement for your Website, and add it to your planning document. Describe the purpose of your Website in a few paragraphs. This will serve as a mission statement for you and others. Try to apply the highest aspirations you can to this mission statement, and then remain committed to them.

Rather than writing, *The purpose of this Website is to sell books,* try, *The purpose of this Website is to sell books efficiently and with the best customer service possible.*

CONSTRUCTION BASICS FOR THE WEB

The present trend is to use scrolling as little as possible, especially on the home page. Even Wells Fargo, with its complex and large-scale operation, manages to get customers anywhere from the home page without requiring them to scroll down a long Web page (although I would recommend that they increase font size for older users, since they have the space to do it). SpectraCom has no scroll bar on the home page, and scrolling is minimal on other pages (and could easily be eliminated).

Designers and writers alike are moving toward a style for home pages where all introductory information can be found without any scrolling. Figure 9.1 shows examples of just some of the home page layout patterns for which I have written text.

Choose the pattern you prefer, and incorporate your own Four Essentials (your front page content). You will have created your basic home page!

As you plan the construction of your Website, here are some points to ponder:

- Books have pages; Websites have pages.
- Books have a clear beginning and end, but Websites are not chronological; each Web page must tie in with *all* others.
- Books always look the same, but content reconfigures on Websites.
- In books readers turn pages; on Websites viewers scroll or hyperlink.
- Newspapers have folds, with important headlines running "over the fold"; Websites have scroll bars, and important content should display without scrolling ("above the fold," so to speak).
- Newspapers have a limited audience, but Websites have a worldwide audience, so be sensitive to jargon which may be misunderstood by a visitor from another country.
- Websites are incorporating video clips more than ever.
- Books don't get published with blank pages that say "Under Construction." If a section of your Website is not complete, don't announce it! Forget putting up a page that says "Under Construction"

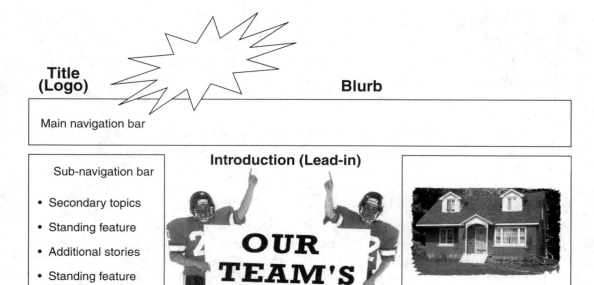

Title
(Logo)

Blurb

Main navigation bar

Sub-navigation bar

- Secondary topics
- Standing feature
- Additional stories
- Standing feature

Introduction (Lead-in)

OUR
TEAM'S
#1

Advertisements

(possibly additional stories
or text-based information)

FIGURE 9.1   Sample home page layout patterns.

or "Coming Soon." Wait until the page is ready and then post it. Why ask viewers to spend time loading a Web page just to tell them that it isn't ready yet?

INTERACTIVITY IS THE HEART OF THE INTERNET

Perhaps more than any other communications medium, the Internet—and specifically the World Wide Web—allows two-way communication between the audience and the presenter. This interactivity is the heart of the Internet.

Books can't do this. Neither can TV or movies. But your Website permits you to involve your viewer in a way that can give him or her a sense of belonging, a feeling of community.

Multimedia is perfect for the writer who can't commit. I'm kidding, of course, but the fact is that multimedia is meant to change. Unlike a book, which is printed and remains the same, content on a Website is meant to

FIGURE 9.1   Continued

change regularly, to be updated and altered. If you don't update your content frequently, your Website will become stale.

Knowledge isn't static. For that matter, life isn't static. Neither is information. Change is inevitable. The strength of multimedia communications is that it is the perfect vehicle for change. Information can be easily updated.

When new questions or developments arise, a Website facilitates new communication. E-mail, feedback forms, message boards, and updated content encourage your audience to view your site as an up-to-date place to learn and interact with others on topics of common interest.

Main navigation bar

Sub-navigation bar

- Secondary topics
- Standing feature
- Additional stories
- Standing feature

Title (Logo)

Introduction (or Lead-in)

Text

_____
_____
_____
_____
_____
_____
_____
_____
_____
_____

Blurb

Graphics or ads

Text _____
_____
_____

FIGURE 9.1   Continued

```
┌─────────────────────────────────────────────────────────────┐
│ Main navigation bar                                           │
└─────────────────────────────────────────────────────────────┘

┌──────────────────────────┐        ✦        ┌──────────────────────────┐
│ Blurb                    │                  │ Introduction (or Lead-in)│
│                          │                  │                          │
└──────────────────────────┘                  └──────────────────────────┘

Text _____
                                                    OUR
_____                                 TEAM'S
        Title                                       #1
        (Logo)
                                              Text

┌──────────────────────┐  ┌──────────────────────────┐    _____
│      Ads             │  │  Sub-navigation bar       │
│                      │  │                           │    _____
│                      │  │  • Secondary topics       │
│   [house image]      │  │                           │    _____
│                      │  │  • Standing feature       │
│                      │  │                           │    _____
│                      │  │  • Additional stories     │
│                      │  │                           │    _____
│                      │  │  • Standing feature       │
└──────────────────────┘  └──────────────────────────┘    _____
```

FIGURE 9.1   Continued

We have a special responsibility not to abuse this privileged communication by:

- being dishonest in the information we present
- talking down or condescending to viewers
- establishing a way for viewers to communicate with us (feedback forms, e-mail, etc.) and then ignoring them when they reach out to us

If we value our viewers as participants rather than objects to be force-fed information, we can learn from them and enlist them as partners in our endeavors.

According to educational psychologist William Glasser, most people absorb 10 percent of what they read, 30 percent of what they see, 70 percent of what they discuss with others, and 95 percent of what they teach someone else. By gearing your Website toward discussion and the exchange of information and ideas, you actually enhance your mission of communication.

Too often, those in the business of designing ads for the Web overwhelm viewers with pop-ups and other annoying, overblown, intrusive techniques. (And they wonder why click-through rates have dropped to record lows on banner-style ads. By 2001, according to industry statistics, the rate of click-throughs had dropped to 0.3 percent.) As reported in the magazine *Business 2.0*, industry insiders may be beginning to realize the problems with such techniques:

> "The first [full-screen] ad we ran for Budweiser took over the page, and people complained," admits Larry Kramer, CEO of San Francisco-based CBS Marketwatch. Since then, "we've said no to ads that intrude too much on the page while you're reading. The trick is to understand what's engaging and what's intrusive."[2]

The worst practice of Website designers is allowing banner ads to predominate over a Website's own content. This trend started because programmers and profiteers decided it was cool, usually without seeking the input of writers, editors, and designers.

As more professional writers, editors, and designers enter the field of multimedia, the trend toward placing ads along the right side of the screen seems to be increasing. Editors, writers, and designers must stand up for the integrity of their content and the dignity of their viewers. I hope that as the mania for profit finds a more reasoned voice, advertising space will be afforded a prominent, but not overpowering, space.

Personally, I don't believe advertising should appear on any home page because this is the top level of content. Ads don't appear on the front of newspapers or magazines because they would diminish the integrity of the publication. Yet Website home pages splash ads above their own content, which may be one reason Web content is viewed with disdain by traditional writers and editors. But that's just my traditional side talking.

Web users don't simply view content; they use the medium to communicate. They are much more active at the computer than when they sit down to watch TV. Unless Web content providers and ad writers understand the interactive nature of the Internet, they actually turn off many of the people they are trying to reach.

Web users will not be forced into passive compliance anymore. They have come to understand and appreciate their own power. Since 1998, I have taught hundreds of people how to use the Internet—from fourth graders to senior citizens as old as 92 years. I have introduced Internet usage to people from at least 20 different countries, and I have seen what happens when they realize that the Web isn't their parents' TV. The 92-year-old gentleman I taught, for example, asked me after two weeks to show him how to recognize ads on Websites so he could avoid them. "They get in my way," he said.

Internet users are activists. They want control, and they want communication. Once they have discovered interactivity, they realize a new personal power. Those who insist on forcing unsolicited information upon them risk alienation.

So how can you utilize interactivity to build communication and earn the respect and interest of viewers?

1. If you establish e-mail or feedback forms, answer them.

2. Present more than just a sales pitch, even if selling is your primary goal. Don't just sell birdhouses. Provide information about which birds use which kind of birdhouses, how to put up birdhouses, how to maintain them, and where to find other helpful Websites with information on birds and birdhouses.

3. Invite viewers to share their experiences—good or bad—with you. Through message boards or monitored chats, give viewers a chance to tell you and others what they think. Which birdhouse works best? Which one fell apart? Through discussion and the exchange of information and ideas, we build true communication and visitor loyalty. Major online players understand this by allowing customers to write reviews of products, evaluate fellow online bidders, or discuss their experiences with travel-service providers and destinations.

4. Maintain your hyperlinks. If links on a Website are outdated or dead, it reflects on the timeliness and credibility of the site and it can be just plain irritating to viewers.

5. Target your message to viewers you know will be interested recipients. It takes more time and effort than simply sticking a blaring online ad in anyone's face, but the long-term effects can be much greater.

6. Update your content regularly, and let your viewers know the last time you updated. Locate a spot on your Website where you report your updates, such as *Site last updated on . . .* , or apply an icon that says *New!* to recently added features. (Don't leave the *New* icon on the feature for longer than a month.)

7. Make sure your content is correct! If viewers visit your Website, they are assuming all the information is honest and correct and that they can count on you. Now legendary is the failure of Toys R Us in 1999 to fill all its Christmas orders—some placed weeks ahead—from online shoppers anxious for their kids to have a great holiday. Media accounts at the time quoted furious parents who vowed never to shop at the site again. The WebMarketingNow.com Newsletter dated January 1, 2000, reported that Toys R Us Chief Executive John Barbour

> sent $100 gift certificates to customers who would not get their merchandise in time for Christmas. However, that didn't patch the feelings many parents felt, which can only be described as rage.

Mike Adams, a single parent, stated he did not receive any notification whatsoever. His repeated phone calls to Toys R Us all ended the same: "on eternal hold." Said Adams, "It wouldn't matter if they sent me a certificate for $1,000. I will never shop at Toys R Us on-line or off-line again. Period."

I am reminded of the time our family had visitors from Australia who wanted to buy sunglasses through an American company while they were visiting here. Before coming from Australia, they had visited the corporate Website and learned that we had a local store that carried the exact style they wanted (unavailable in Australia.) So we went to the store only to be told by the manager that "just because it's on our Website, doesn't mean it's true. We don't carry that style here. You really should have called first." I explained that their content provider should have thought better of posting the inaccurate information on the corporate site. We left without sunglasses and never shopped there again.

HOW EDUCATIONAL THEORY APPLIES TO YOUR VIEWERS

With the development of computers that are small enough to fit in classrooms and powerful enough to perform a variety of functions, education has had to investigate the effects of this technology and its potential uses. A leading theory linking technology and learning is called Constructivism. We can adapt parts of this theory to our communication not just with students but with clients, employees, customers, and the public at large.

Below are some primary tenets of Constructivism. (They have *a lot* to do with interactivity.)

1. *Content must be relevant and timely to viewers.* If a Website has content that is outdated or inapplicable to the audience it purports to serve, it will lose viewership. Unlike a book, which is complete the moment it is printed, a Website is born the moment it goes live. It must be updated on a regular basis, and efforts must be made to keep content relevant to intended viewers.

2. *Seek and value viewers' opinions and ideas.* As stated earlier, the gift of the Web is its inherent interactivity. For a Website to exist without encouraging feedback and communication from viewers is a waste of the medium.

3. *There is more than one way to interpret information.* The Web is open to an international audience of people from all walks of life and many cultures. Be aware that how you view and present information is open to wide interpretation based on the life experiences of those who visit your site.

4. *Learning is a dynamic process.* In the traditional classroom (and in traditional advertising and copywriting), recipients of information were expected to sit passively and have information "poured" into their brains. But with the advent of the Web, students and customers can react, provide input, and build their own learning experiences. Viewers decide what information they wish to collect from a Website by clicking on links. It is a much different information-gathering experience than reading a book and turning pages chronologically.

5. *Encourage viewers to develop their own solutions.* With the Web, there are multiple sources of information readily available on a single subject. Through external links, Websites provide more points of view than can exist on any one Website. The days of one book or one teacher or one advertiser acting as sole authority are gone. Within minutes, people can compare prices, data, claims, facts, and ideas to build their own knowledge and solutions. Power and control belong to both those who publish Websites and those who view them. A Website or Web ad that facilitates rather than dictates is more appropriate.

In conclusion, the best use of the Web occurs when viewers are allowed to respond to what they have seen and consider what they have learned in the context of their own experience and knowledge. Viewers need to be encouraged to interact with one another as well as with those who publish information. Viewers need to be respected for their innate intelligence and permitted to act as researchers and participants in the Web experience. Content can be a mechanism to provide leadership, mentoring, and encouragement rather than a one-way, autocratic, force-feed information delivery system.

Traditional advertising models that have been imposed on the Web are not proving effective over the long run. According to well-established learning theories, this is probably because the assumptions are based on those developed for TV and movie trailers, where viewers sit as passive observers (much as they have for years in traditional classrooms and religious sanctuaries). In those environments, people expect to be spoon-fed information and told what conclusions to draw by external forces: the teacher, the preacher, the advertiser, the marketer, the news anchor.

But on the Web, they don't have to click on the banner ad. They don't have to stay on one Web page. They don't have to wait for the obnoxious pop-up ad to load. Viewers quickly develop a variety of self-initiated ways to plan and pursue objectives, gather and discern information, and optimize their own learning experiences.

To reach and keep these self-motivated, self-directed viewers, traditional external forces—the teacher, the preacher, the advertiser, the marketer, the doctor, the boss—need to develop a less authoritative and more facilitative role, particularly when communicating text on the Web.

As you develop content for the Web, ask yourself if the copy is designed to:

Shock	or	Enlighten
Direct	or	Guide
Impose	or	Facilitate
Dictate	or	Clarify

The first group of words is tradition-based (TV, print, radio), while the second group of words is multimedia-based and properly geared toward interactivity.

When you write content, do you think of your viewers as:

Compliant	or	Independent
Obedient	or	Curious
Rigid	or	Flexible
Predictable	or	Creative
Homogeneous	or	Unique
Average	or	Intelligent

Too many traditional market research studies and focus groups are based on finding commonalities, which may work well for traditional media. But judging from the variety of people I have taught to use the Internet, one would do well to recognize people's individualities and widely varying methods of exploring Websites. Whereas different people can pretty much be counted on to sit in front of a TV screen and laugh at a preprogrammed, laugh track–enhanced comedy show in much the same way, few people click on the same hyperlinks or utilize Website information in the same manner.

Through my teaching, I have found Internet users to be independent, curious, flexible, creative, unique, and intelligent beings. While they may initially come into the classroom expecting a TV-style experience, they soon grow and expand to the point where they can actively compare the quality of information on various Websites, avoid annoying ads, and find a user comfort zone based on their own life experiences. One size does not fit all when it comes to writing for Web users.

UTILIZING HYPERLINKS

If interactivity is the key to Websites and CD-ROMs, hyperlinks are the key to interactivity. In the mid-1990s when I worked as an editor for a start-up search engine, we put hyperlinks into everything. We wrote tutorials and features in which every other word was a hyperlink to a different Website. But as time passed, we began to realize that this was hyperlink abuse. Too many hyperlinks stuck in the middle of a sentence can destroy a viewer's train of thought and ruin flow. With each sentence, a viewer linked to a different Website, then had to find a way back to the sentence—while trying to remember what the sentence said to begin with, which was tricky.

Today, it is more common to place hyperlinks in their own space rather than to drop them willy-nilly into general content. Placing links at the end of your content rather than scattering them throughout is preferable. Place links at the end of an article under a heading such as *Related links* or *To learn more, visit these sites.* (See examples of this by clicking on stories at the Environmental News Network Website, enn.com.)

Another option is to open hyperlinked Websites in their own window. (See examples of this in the *Find Tools and Resources* section of the Special Species Website, www.specialspecies.com.) To make sure viewers realize they are no longer on your site, have the external Websites open in separate, overlapping windows. Viewers can easily click out of those windows to return to your site. This increases usability and makes it clear to viewers that the content comes from a Website other than your own.

When you use a hyperlink, make sure it adds to the overall value of your content and isn't a distraction from your message. Choosing external Websites to include as hyperlinks on your own Website is a matter requiring great care. The last thing you want to do is send your viewers off to another site with questionable information. Even though you didn't write the material yourself, it will still reflect on your credibility and that of your Website. If in doubt, leave it out. Don't link to another site just because it's clever or has a slick, fancy design.

Review

1. Try to apply the highest aspirations you can to your mission statement, and then remain committed to them.
2. Unlike a book, which is printed and remains the same, content on a Website is meant to change regularly.
3. E-mail, feedback forms, message boards, and updated content encourage your audience to view your site as an up-to-date place to learn and interact with others on topics of common interest.
4. Perhaps more than any other communications medium, the Internet—and specifically the World Wide Web—allows two-way communication between the audience and the presenter.
5. By gearing your Website toward discussion and the exchange of information and ideas, you actually enhance your mission of communication.
6. Internet users are activists. They want control, and they want communication. Once they have discovered interactivity, they realize a new personal power. Those who insist on forcing unsolicited information upon them risk alienation.

Key Terms and Concepts

Interactivity   Communication among people using the tools of the Internet.

Internet   A global network of computers that allows confidential and nonclassified files of information to be transmitted and shared worldwide.

Scrolling   Using a navigation device to roll up or down a long Web page.

Usability   The ease with which a Website is navigated and understood.

World Wide Web   One aspect of the Internet that contains primarily nonclassified governmental, commercial, educational, and organizational electronic files displayed within constructs called Websites.

Chapter Questions

1. What are six ways you can utilize interactivity to build communication and earn the respect and interest of viewers?
2. What are five basic tenets of Constructivism?

Now You Try

Part A

1. Go on the Web. Look at the titles of five Websites. Evaluate them to determine which are clear and which are unclear or confusing. Notice where the titles are placed on the home page and the words that are used. Do you understand immediately what each Website is about based on the word or words used? Explain why or why not.
2. Go on the Web. Look at the lead headlines on five Websites. Evaluate whether or not you think they are clear and effective. Explain your point of view.

Part B

On the CD-ROM, visit the recommended Helpful Websites for chapter 9 to find:

- Web writing researcher Jakob Nielsen's many credible articles, studies, tips, insights, and resources
- An article on the impact of the Internet on teaching and learning

Write 15 interesting facts you learned from visiting these Websites. Identify where each fact came from (by Website title and Web page address).

Part C

On the CD-ROM, open the "Crafting Multimedia Text" folder, and click "Plan Website Text." Complete this section.

Unconventional Wisdom

- Web pages are written to be sampled, not read cover to cover.
- When you publish a book, you have finished writing it; when you publish a Website, you've just begun writing it.

Endnotes

1. *The Columbia world of quotations.* (1996). New York: Columbia University Press. Retrieved on January 28, 2004, from www.bartleby.com/66/87/1687.html.
2. Gaffney, J. (2002, June). The online advertising comeback. *Business 2.0.* 118–120.

Answers for Chapter 9

Chapter Questions

1. ***What are six ways you can utilize interactivity to build communication and earn the respect and interest of viewers?***

1. If you establish e-mail or feedback forms, answer them.

2. Present more than just a sales pitch, even if selling is your primary goal. Don't just sell birdhouses. Provide information about which birds use which kind of birdhouses, how to put up birdhouses, how to maintain them, and where to find other helpful Websites with information on birds and birdhouses.

3. Invite viewers to share their experiences—good or bad—with you. Through message boards or monitored chats, give viewers a chance to tell you and others what they think. Which birdhouse works best? Which one fell apart?

4. Maintain your hyperlinks. If links on a Website are outdated or dead, it reflects on the timeliness and credibility of the site and it can be just plain irritating to viewers.

5. Target your message to viewers you know will be interested recipients. It takes more time and effort than simply sticking a blaring online ad in anyone's face, but the long-term effects can be much greater.

6. Update your content regularly, and let your viewers know the last time you updated.

2. ***What are five basic tenets of Constructivism?***

1. Content must be relevant and timely to viewers. If a Website has content that is outdated or inapplicable to the audience it purports to serve, it will lose viewership.

2. Seek and value viewers' opinions and ideas. As stated earlier, the gift of the Web is its inherent interactivity. For a Website to exist without encouraging feedback and communication from viewers is a waste of the medium.

3. There is more than one way to interpret information. The Web is open to an international audience of people from all walks of life and many cultures. Be aware that how you view and present information is open to wide interpretation based on the life experiences of those who visit your site.

4. Learning is a dynamic process. In the traditional classroom (and in traditional advertising and copywriting), recipients of information were expected to sit passively and have information "poured" into their brains. But with the advent of the Web, students and customers can react, provide input, and build their own learning experiences.

5. Encourage viewers to develop their own solutions. With the Web, there are multiple sources of information readily available on a single subject. Through external links, Websites provide more points of view than can exist on any one Website. The days of one book or one teacher or one advertiser acting as sole authority are gone. Within minutes, people can compare prices, data, claims, facts, and ideas to build their own knowledge and solutions.

Special Considerations for Visual Presentations

Words are, of course, the most powerful drug used by mankind.

—Rudyard Kipling[1]

OBJECTIVES

This chapter will help you learn:

- An effective way to construct a good script
- Final tips to enliven your audience

AN EFFECTIVE WAY TO CONSTRUCT A GOOD SCRIPT

The ability to present text visually is now constantly expanding through iMovie, CD-ROM burners, Authorware, AppleWorks, Apple Keynote, and Microsoft PowerPoint just to name a few options. (See Appendix A for information about different types of useful multimedia software for the writer.)

Many business and classroom presentations these days are built using Microsoft PowerPoint, and, more recently, Apple Keynote. These allow you to present text on the "big screen" with special colors, effects, and graphics. They provide a very fun and fancy way to liven up a speech or present a report to a group. And now, presentations can be easily uploaded to Websites or burned onto CD-ROMs for people to view on their own.

Here are two Websites that routinely make outstanding use of slide presentations:

- Pain.com (www.pain.com) posts lectures and slide shows for professionals and for patient education purposes.
- SignOnSanDiego.com (www.signonsandiego.com/gallery), the Website for the *San Diego Union-Tribune*, posts photographic slide presentations of local, national, and international news. During the terrible wildfires that devastated much of rural San Diego County in fall 2003, this Website maintained updated photos showing the public where the fires were advancing and what damage had been done. The photos were organized into slide presentations by category and were easy to locate and use.

To see some other ways people have uploaded PowerPoint-style presentations to the Web, visit:

- "Tropical Cloud Forests: Introduction to their Diversity and Ecology," "An On-line Course for Teachers Produced by the College of Exploration, Dr. Jason Bradford, and colleagues from the Andes Biodiversity Consortium" at coexploration.org/biodiversity/html/pptdemo/v3dcmnt.htm
- "Multimedia Communications: Writing and Display Principles," (multimedia writing geared to general public) at userwww.sfsu.edu/%7Ebmoran/HTML%20FINAL/tsld001.htm
- "Operation TeddyCare: What Do We Do?" (pictorial slide show for trauma counselors to use with kids) at teddycare.coastside.net/whatwedo.html
- "Sheridan Patrol PowerPoint Show" (keeping kids safe in Spokane, WA) at www.spokaneschools.org/Sheridan/watch_the_sheridan_patrol_powerp.htm
- "Add a Little SPICE (& HERBS) to Your Life!" Food Tips/Recipe Ideas from the University of Nebraska's Cooperative Extension in Lancaster Country (edited and updated by Alice Henneman, MS, RD, & Extension Educator) at lancaster.unl.edu/food/spiceherb.htm#powerpoint

But however you choose to use a slide presentation, the most important aspect is still the script. It needs to be well written before any colors or other effects are added.

The script is very simply all the words. The script is not colors, backgrounds, graphics, or special effects. It is words, text, copy, written content.

When Hollywood makes a movie, it starts with words. The script is produced on paper, and all the visuals are created later. A TV show starts with a written script. A presentation is a show, too. It needs to start with a written script as well.

The Scripting Process

Some presentation software programs offer an outline view, which gives you the opportunity to write your script in outline form. Another way is to open PowerPoint and write your slides with no colors, no backgrounds, or other effects. Just get your words down on each slide. You will go back later and (in this order, preferably):

1. resize and arrange your words on each slide
2. add colored backgrounds and text
3. choose fonts or word art
4. insert motion and sound effects
5. place pictures, charts, or other graphics

Once you have written your script in black letters on a white background, make a printout for editing purposes. Go to "Handouts" or "Slides" and print out four to six slides per page. Let the project sit for a while, and then, armed with a pencil, read over your script carefully. Add or subtract words until you are happy with the script. Show it to your coworkers or supervisor to get their input as well.

Make final edits in PowerPoint before you add any "extras." This technique allows you to really pay attention to what you are saying and how you are saying it before you incorporate effects that might hide omissions or weaknesses in the content. When I teach PowerPoint, I never allow my students to add any colors or effects until they have written their scripts and turned them in to me in good old black and white. The words must be carefully considered; then add the bells and whistles. When you really look at the words in your script, it helps you better choose appropriate colors, font styles, and effects.

Absolutely do a spelling and grammar check at this point. A typographical error in a written report may be overlooked, but the same error projected onto a giant screen becomes very obvious.

Another way to tackle the scripting process is to write your script in pencil on white, lined or unlined 4- × 6-inch cards. Each card represents a slide.

No matter what scripting method you use, because you have a multimedia presentation, review and update it frequently.

Attention to every detail is important. Don't forget that grammar, spelling, and punctuation:

- Reflect upon your message, professionalism, confidence, and training
- Affect the credibility of the *whole* presentation
- Reflect upon you as author and your company or organization

---

When dealing with content, first decide: What's the goal? (Sum it up in one paragraph, a "nut graph.") Who is your audience (industry insiders, older people, friends, customers, teens etc.)? Then

- Gather information and ideas.
- Write out information and ideas (on cards or using a software application).
- Group related information and ideas.
- Organize sections in order of importance (with important things first).
- Prepare a rough draft (organize your script).
- Write up your presentation in its intended form.
- Leave it for a while, and come back to it later.
- Do editing (if possible, have someone else review it with you).

Exploration

Turn the passage below into a script for a slide presentation. Get 15 to 20 4- × 6-inch cards. Separate the information in the following passage into individual facts, and organize them onto the cards as if each card represented one slide. (See one recommended script on pages 215–218.) This will give you practice writing a script from a fact sheet. Making a fact sheet first is another good way to make sure you have covered all the information you need to include.

Attracting wild birds to your yard can be a fun and environmentally helpful activity. It doesn't take a lot of time or money. Birds need what people need—shelter, food, and water. If you can supply some or all of these things, you will have birds visit you. To provide shelter, you can plant dense bushes or put in a tree. Native plants and trees are best because birds in your area evolved with them. A native plant is one that grows naturally in an area and has not been brought in or introduced from somewhere else. Or you can hang a birdhouse. To provide water, buy a birdbath. Or put a shallow pan of water on your balcony railing. You can even turn a garbage can lid upside down and put a brick in the middle of it. Never fill any container deeper than 2 inches because birds can drown. Add rocks if the bottom is slippery. And keep the water clean. To provide food, you can put out a bird feeder. Different kinds of birds like different kinds of seeds. American goldfinches, for example, like niger seed. Other finches like black oil sunflower seeds. Some birds are attracted to peanuts, fruit, or suet. Or you can put in plants that have fruits birds like, or attract insects birds like to eat. Make sure your bird paradise is safe from cats. Don't place a feeder or birdbath where cats can easily hide. You can learn a lot about birds in your area and what they need by visiting the National Audubon Society's Website at www.audubon.org. According to the society, "more than one-quarter of America's birds are in trouble or decline" (such as the painted bunting), so why not see how you can help today?

Remember, It's the Law

Just because your words are not on paper does not mean they are exempt from copyright laws. You own what you write in most cases, no matter how your text is presented—on paper or on screen.

Copyright laws apply to multimedia; you can't cut and paste content without giving credit, or you will commit plagiarism.

You should also copyright your own work to protect it. Place the copyright year along with your name or company on the title page of your slide show. (See chapter 4 to review other copyright legalities.)

You have no right to copy and paste anyone else's words or images into your presentation without supplying attribution. Your last slide should always be a resource slide that lists where you obtained any information, particularly quotes and copyrighted images.

FINAL TIPS TO ENLIVEN YOUR PRESENTATION

Most slide presentation software provides layout schemes from which you may choose. It is important, however, not to overuse the layout templates or make your slide shows longer than 20 to 35 slides (the closer to 20 the better), or your audience may become bored or fidgety. The standard backgrounds are used so often that they sometimes come with their own automatic boredom factor. Use them only when you are in a great hurry or if you have never learned how to design your own.

In PowerPoint, for example, you can create your own design by looking under "Format." You have many options for creating original color schemes, layouts, and designs. (And it's fun!) Start by formatting your own backgrounds and fonts. PowerPoint offers you a menu of choices featuring one-column, two-column, and multi-column selections with spaces set aside for clip art and images.

But rather than always relying on the template designs and layouts, try creating your own backgrounds and styles. Use text boxes and other tricks to vary how each slide looks. With PowerPoint, you can choose a blank slide, then go to Insert>Text box. Press and drag to make your own box for text. Type in words and move the box wherever you would like it to appear on your slide.

Visual Impact

As I emphasized earlier in this book, visual impact is much more important in multimedia than in traditional printed reports, books, or other text-based documents. See chapters 4 and 7 to review in depth what is covered below.

Go for contrast. What looks good on your computer screen may wash out on a projector screen. Light background with dark text—and vice versa—will work best.

Fonts you choose may not be available on the computer you use for your presentation. Always have a dress rehearsal to check fonts, contrast, timing, and so on.

Keep shows shorter than 36 slides, or provide an intermission. If you have a lot of words:

- Don't crowd them. They are hard to read.
- Break up text (with bullets, color, emphasis).
- If you must crowd words, allow time for people to read and comprehend them. For example, take antidisestablishmentarianism—large words take longer to read.
- Try to leave lots of space between lines.

Contrast Issues

Your audience will have to look straight ahead or up to view your words. They will be seated much farther away from the words than if they were reading a book. They will have to contend with glare or with "washout" that occurs when a presentation is projected onto a screen. Resolution is lost, which is why paying attention to font size and color contrast is so important.

The color of words gives impact. Make sure colors are aesthetically pleasing. If you have a dark background, make your letters light-colored (for example, dark blue background with light yellow letters). If you have a light background, make your letters dark (for example, light pink background with dark purple letters). So often, a color combination looks good on the computer screen but completely washes out when it is projected onto a screen for an audience. Your presentation will seem amateurish if your audience cannot see your content.

Here's a good way to determine if you have enough contrast in your PowerPoint show. Put your slides into "Slide Sorter" view. Then take two giant steps back from your computer screen and look at your slides. If some of your words are "washing" into the background and becoming difficult to see, you have contrast or font size work to do.

Readability Issues

Don't use font sizes smaller than 28 points. They are too hard to read from a distance. And don't use charts or graphs from print documents that are too small to discern on-screen. Either build a chart specifically for your on-screen presentation or hand out the charts on paper.

Never put yourself in the position of apologizing to your audience because you know they can't see some aspect of your presentation. If some element is too small to see, don't include it. Or fix it!

Other Reminders

The type of font you use affects the viewers and mood of your presentation.

The font size determines the importance of the words. You generally notice bigger words before smaller ones. In addition to size, other techniques for emphasis include:

1. Putting text in **boldface**
2. *Putting text in italics*
3. Changing a portion of text to a **different font**
4. <u>Underlining text</u>
5. Moving text (animation)

6. Putting text in ALL CAPITAL letters (which can be perceived as "shouting" at your audience if you overdo it)

Effective Emphasis

Don't overuse <u>emphasis techniques.</u> CHOOSE what you use **carefully** and with **thought.**

Or *your* presentation will look confusing, *messy,* and <u>unprofessional</u>. A LITTLE goes a long way. (See?)

How you place words on a slide gives them importance, too. Words or phrases that stand alone seem more important than those in a list or column.

One educational theory that has gained wide acceptance over the years involves the primacy and recency effects. Simply stated, people tend to remember the first and last items in a list much better than items in the middle of a list. More attention is available early on, and less mental interference occurs near the end. So if you have a number of items you wish your audience to remember, put your most essential information first and summarize well at the end.

Try to offer information in clearly grouped chunks. Let the audience thoroughly absorb one chunk or block of information before presenting the next.

Keep sentences short, crisp, and clear. It is OK to use phrases rather than complete sentences. Instead of writing, *Here is a list of all of our upcoming new color lines for fall*, write *New fall color lines.*

And instead of putting on a slide, *Here is a thorough analysis of our latest sales figures for the month of October*, put this: *Latest October Sales Figures.* You can supplement with handouts if you need to go into a lot of detail later.

Exploration

Preserving their meaning, turn these sentences into the kinds of phrases you might find on a slide in a presentation. (Possible answers are on page 215, but try it yourself first.)

1. Here are some interesting facts about different kinds of roses.
2. The various kinds of roses can be put into these categories.
3. There are things you need to remember about pruning roses.
4. Roses need certain conditions to grow and look their best.
5. If you go onto the Internet you can visit these Websites for more information.

How To Present

Avoid using too many sound effects because you will have to read over them. And, yes, it is considered important that you read your content to your audience loudly enough to be heard. Ask if there are any questions along the way. Use your presentation as a guideline for points you wish to address, rather than as a script from which you cannot deviate.

A major boredom factor can be the length of a presentation. If your presentation is longer than 35 slides, provide an intermission. Take questions, turn on the lights, and give the audience a chance to get up and move around. When you reconvene, allow people a few minutes to get back into the show by offering a quick review of key points covered to that point. This can be the first slide you show following the break.

Don't set your presentation on an automatic timer. If one audience member has a question, by the time you finish answering it, your slide show will be over. Maintain control of your presentation by using mouse clicks or other techniques that allow you to start or stop at will.

Don't rush through your presentation. Interference theory contends that forgetting occurs when people are not given enough time to "mentally rehearse" new information. This is why it is important to repeat major points of a presentation in summary slides if possible before you move on to new and different points. You are in charge of how much time your viewers have to read your text, so don't rush them. This is another reason why you need to read your text aloud for your audience. It helps you estimate how long it is taking people to read and digest your words. Speak slowly, clearly, and distinctly. Encourage questions.

As we discussed in other parts of this book, try to use an active, personal tone. If humor is appropriate, include it. Stylize your writing to fit your subject and your audience. People will respond better if they feel that you are talking to them, not reading at them. Incorporate the "you" word and make eye contact even if you are in a dark room. Be friendly.

Your audience must overcome distractions created within the room itself. People may be walking in and out, for example, or whispering to one another. The air-conditioning unit may be rattling. The room may be too hot. The chairs might squeak. Be attentive to your audience and the need to maintain control of the room. Tell people when there will be a break so they don't just get up and walk out during your presentation. Request that cell phones be turned off.

Don't be autocratic, but do be authoritative. The audience needs you to be in charge. Your audience must overcome a lot to stick with you, so try to help them stay focused as much as possible. Unless they need to take notes, dim the lights to make it easier to see the projector screen.

If you are presenting information they will need later, announce at the beginning that you will be providing handouts. This way, audience members won't need to try and take notes in the dark. But don't distribute the handouts until the end. People will attempt to read them in the dark or they may just take the handouts and leave.

Presenting Like a Pro

- Don't use a timer on your presentation. It's better to set the pace with the mouse in case you get questions from the audience.
- Don't speak too softly or not at all. Always read your presentation aloud to your audience in a pleasant tone.
- Don't rush. Give your audience time to absorb each slide and ask questions.

Before you present, try to rehearse your presentation in the room with the computer you will use. See if any fonts have defaulted. (If the computer you are using does not have the same fonts as the computer on which you wrote your show, it will choose a default font.)

Have someone sit in the back of the room. Practice delivering your text. Make sure you can be heard when you speak, but don't shout. Above all, be prepared. Whatever can go wrong probably will! Have handouts of your show ready to distribute just in case the projector bulb blows, or the power fails, or your laptop battery dies, or—well, you get the picture.

Exploration

Find a poem you like. Read it in front of a group. Pay attention to making eye contact, reading with "feeling," and speaking forcefully enough to be heard at the back of the room. Have your audience offer suggestions, and then read the poem aloud again.

Review

1. No matter how you choose to use a slide presentation, the most important aspect is the script.
2. The script needs to be well written before any colors or other effects are added.
3. Just get your words down on each slide. You will go back later and (in this order, preferably) resize and arrange your words on each slide; add colored backgrounds and text; choose fonts or word art; insert motion and sound effects; and place pictures, charts, or other graphics.

4. Once you have written your script in black letters on a white background, make a printout for editing purposes. Go to "Handouts" or "Slides," and print out four to six slides per page.
5. Let the project sit for a while; then, armed with a pencil, add or subtract words until you are happy with your script.
6. Show it to your coworkers or supervisor to get their input as well.
7. Make final edits in PowerPoint before you add any "extras."
8. Always do a spelling and grammar check.
9. When you really look at the words in your script, it helps you better choose appropriate colors, font styles, and effects.
10. Because you have a multimedia presentation, you can and should review and update it frequently.
11. Just because your words are not on paper does not mean they are exempt from copyright laws. You have every right to copyright your slide presentations.
12. You have no right to copy and paste anyone else's words or images into your presentation without supplying attribution.
13. Your last slide should always be a resource slide that explains where you got any information or images for your show.
14. Don't overuse templates or make your slide show longer than 25 to 35 slides.
15. A color combination may look good on the computer screen but completely "wash out" when it is projected onto a screen for an audience.
16. Your presentation will seem amateurish if your audience cannot see your content.
17. Never put yourself in the position of apologizing to your audience because you know they can't see some aspect of your presentation.
18. Avoid using too many sound effects because you will have to read over them.
19. It is important that you read your content to your audience loudly enough to be heard.
20. Ask if there are any questions along the way.
21. Use your presentation as a guideline for points you wish to address, rather than as a script from which you cannot deviate.
22. If your presentation is longer than 35 slides, provide an intermission.
23. Don't set your slide show on an automatic timer.
24. Don't rush through your presentation.
25. Interference theory contends that forgetting occurs when people are not given enough time to "mentally rehearse" new information.
26. Put your most essential information first, and summarize well at the end.
27. Try to offer information in clearly grouped chunks.
28. Keep sentences short, crisp, and clear. It is OK to use phrases.

29. People respond better if they feel that you are talking to them, not reading at them.
30. Your audience must overcome distractions created within the room itself.
31. The audience needs you to be in charge.
32. Rehearse your presentation in the room with the computer you will use.

Key Terms and Concepts

Fact sheet   A written document containing all the information that must be included in a presentation's script.

Resource slide   The final presentation slide that lists all the sources or sites from which information or images were taken.

Script   All the words in your presentation.

Chapter Questions

1. What are three ways to make sure you have effective contrast on your slides?
2. What are three things to remember when you present to an audience?

Now You Try

Part A

On the CD-ROM, visit the recommended Helpful Websites for chapter 10 to find:

- Information on visual, slide show–style presentations, suggestions for preparation and development, design guidelines, and advice for putting it all together

Write 15 interesting facts you learned from visiting this Website.

Part B

On the CD-ROM, open the "Crafting Multimedia Text" folder, and click "Plan Presentation Text." Complete this section.

Unconventional Wisdom

- Try to avoid font sizes smaller than 28 points.
- Strive for thoughtful, concise content.
- If you have more than 35 slides, provide an intermission.
- It's called a slide *show,* not a slide *report stuck on a screen*.
- Use the mouse, not the timer, between slides.

Endnote

1. *The Columbia world of quotations.* (1996.) New York: Columbia University Press.

Answers for Chapter 10

Exploration

In answer to the exercise on page 207, here's one possible script that could have been written on 15 cards, equaling 15 slides.

Title Slide:
Are You for the Birds?

Slide #2:
Did you know
• "more than one-quarter of America's birds are in trouble or decline"?
— National Audubon Society

Slide #3:
Birds
• Fill our lives with song
• Eat pesty bugs and insects
• Are fun to watch

Slide #4:
Do we really want to lose them?

Slide #5:
No! So what can we do?

Slide #6:
Birds need what people need:
• Shelter
• Food
• Water

Slide #7:
Shelter for birds
Plant dense bushes or trees. Natives are best. They evolved locally and birds evolved with them.

Slide #8:
Put up a birdhouse. Different birds use different kinds.

Slide #9:
Water for birds
Buy a birdbath.
Make a birdbath.
		Try a garbage can lid turned upside down with a brick in the middle.

Slide #10:
Fill a shallow pan:
• Never deeper than 2 inches.
• Add rocks so birds don't drown.

Slide #11:
Food for birds
Hang a bird feeder.
Different birds like different seeds.
- American goldfinches: niger
- Other finches: black oil sunflower seeds
- Other birds: peanuts, fruit, or suet

Slide #12:
Put in bird-friendly plants.
- Fruit bearers
- Plants that attract insects that birds will find yummy

Slide #13:
Make sure whatever you do is safe from cats!

Slide #14:
Discover:
- Birds in your area
- What they need to survive

Slide #15:
Visit the National Audubon Society:
www.audubon.org

The birds will thank you with a song.

Exploration

Below are possible answers to the exercise on page 210.

1. Different kinds of roses

2. Rose categories

3. Pruning tips

4. What roses need to thrive

5. To learn more, visit:

Chapter Questions

1. ***What are three ways to make sure you have effective contrast on your slides?***

   Colors, font size, spacing.

2. ***What are three things to remember when you present to an audience? (Here are 17.)***

   1. Avoid using too many sound effects because you will have to read over them.

   2. Read your content to your audience loudly enough to be heard.

   3. Encourage questions.

   4. Use your presentation as a guideline for points you wish to address, rather than as a script from which you cannot deviate.

   5. If your presentation is longer than 35 slides, provide an intermission.

   6. Don't set your presentation on an automatic timer.

   7. Don't rush through your presentation.

   8. Repeat major points of a presentation in summary slides.

   9. Speak slowly, clearly, and distinctly.

   10. Try to use an active, personal tone.

   11. If humor is appropriate, use it. Be friendly.

   12. Be attentive to your audience and the need to maintain control of the room.

   13. Unless they need to take notes, dim the lights to make it easier for audience members to see the projector screen.

   14. If you are relating information they will need later, announce at the beginning that you will be providing handouts.

   15. Don't distribute the handouts until the end.

   16. Before you present, rehearse your presentation in the room with the computer you will use.

   17. Be prepared. Whatever can go wrong, probably will!

Appendix A

Great (Writer-Friendly) Software for Websites and Presentations

WEBSITES

When people think about building Websites, they often think about programs such as Microsoft FrontPage or Macromedia Dreamweaver (which is really considered the state-of-the-art Web design program these days). But these programs can be complicated and require more coding than a writer wants—or needs—to learn. Here are some interesting alternatives for writers:

Microsoft Word

Most writers think of MS Word as a word-processing tool for print writing. But it can also be used to construct a basic Website, which is a valuable tool if you want to share content with a designer or lay out your text yourself. Recent versions of Word let you save documents as HTML coded documents (File>Save as Web Page) and open your Web documents to keep working on them (File>Open Web Page). There is also a Web Page Preview feature. So you can write your content as if you were just creating a Word document, but then save it as a Web page and let Word do the HTML coding for you. It's not perfect, but for writers it's a welcome start. Finally, Word also has Web page templates, so you can pick a design and put in your own content. In the Project Gallery (or New) area, you will find blank Web pages or Web page templates. Don't get too creative with the templates, however, by changing font sizes or styles radically, or the templates don't work very well. MS Word is frequently sold as part of MS Office, which also contains MS PowerPoint. There are Windows and Mac versions. To see how to build a simple Website using MS Word, visit my link at online.sfsu.edu/~bmoran/Moran/ Website/index.html. (It is geared to teachers, but the process is the same for anyone.)

Netscape Composer

Netscape is not just a Web browser but also a program that allows you to construct a simple Website. Just open Netscape, and look under Window on the toolbar to find Composer. It opens a blank form that writes HTML for you as you create your text. Make generous use of the Help section if you need to. Or visit my link at online.sfsu.edu/~bmoran/Moran/Website/index.html to see how to build a basic Website using Composer.

Yahoo/GeoCities

Yahoo offers a Web hosting service (and other services) for small businesses at smallbusiness.yahoo.com/index.php. You do not have to be a Web design expert to get a business Website. You provide the content, pay a fee, and Yahoo does the rest for you. So as a writer or small-business owner, you can have a real presence on the Web just by providing great content.

Adobe Acrobat

You can find out more about how Adobe PDFs work and how to use Adobe Acrobat software at www.adobe.com. Depending on how you use it, you can make any document a PDF file that is uneditable or that, with your approval, lets others open, edit, and/or write comments in the file by using their own Web browsers. You create Adobe PDF files by clicking buttons, and it is not very complicated. The current version is Adobe Acrobat 6.0, available for Macintosh and Windows. Adobe PDF files preserve the look of your original documents, and you can share them with anyone, regardless of hardware and software platforms. Unless e-mail attachments may contain viruses when opened, PDF files are safe to open and view. See examples of Adobe Acrobat PDF file downloads at the U.S. Copyright Office Web page, located at www.copyright.gov/title17. Later versions of MS Word and Quark let you create PDF files.

Adobe Reader

You must have Adobe Reader to view Adobe Acrobat PDF files. The good news is it's free! You can download it right from the Web at the Adobe Web page located at www.adobe.com/products/acrobat/readstep2.html.

PRESENTATIONS

When people think about building visual presentations, they often think about programs such as Macromedia Authorware or Apple's Final Cut Pro. But these programs can be complicated and require more training than a writer wants—or needs.

The world of visual presentations is rapidly evolving from basic slide shows to movies and interactive presentations that writers can build themselves. Even kids make iMovies, and if they can do it, so can we. Here are some interesting alternatives for writers:

Microsoft PowerPoint

Still considered the standard-bearer for slide presentations, this program lets you fashion professional-looking slides easily; edit them in collaboration with others; and then either show them on a projector screen, transfer them to a CD-ROM, or upload them to the Web. MS PowerPoint is frequently sold as part of MS Office, which also contains MS Word. There are Windows and Mac versions. To see a fun, if somewhat outdated, tutorial on how to use PowerPoint, visit PowerPoint in the Classroom at www.actden.com/pp. (It's geared to kids so it's not too intimidating.)

Apple Keynote

This is Apple's challenge to PowerPoint, and it's so new that I'm reserving judgment. To see a thorough overview of the program and what it can do, visit the Keynote section of the Apple Website at www.apple.com/keynote. It does look impressive, but I need more time to really put it to the test.

iMovie

This is an Apple product with which I am very familiar, and I think it's great. I have used it with schoolchildren, teachers, and businesspeople, and it has always proven a fun and rewarding experience. You can scan images, take videos, or insert digital camera shots without trouble and then write titles, create transitions, and add music. Unlike a slide show that clicks along, iMovies flow. To read more about iMovie, visit Apple at www.apple.com/imovie. The best part is that iMovie often comes free with other Apple programs or with new Apple computers. There's a good iMovie tutorial at etc.sccoe.k12.ca.us/i2000/00mod/1_mm/imov.html. To see what kids have created with iMovie, check out www.apple.com/education/dv/gallery.

MS Moviemaker

This is Microsoft's challenge to iMovie, and it's so new that I'm reserving judgment. To see a thorough overview of the program and what it can do, visit the Moviemaker section of the Microsoft Website at www.microsoft.com/windowsxp/moviemaker/default.asp. It does look writer-friendly, but I need more time to really put it to the test.

Appendix B

Finding Help Along the Way:
Additional Reading About Writing

To develop even more confidence about multimedia writing, here is helpful reading material (and be sure to visit Websites contained on the CD-ROM):

BOOKS ABOUT WRITING AND LANGUAGE ARTS

Junk English by Ken Smith, Blast Books (humorous guide to empty rhetoric and pliable, flabby language) ISBN 0922233233

Edwin Newman on Language: Strictly Speaking/A Civil Tongue/Complete in One Volume Galahad Books (geared primarily to journalists) ASIN 0883657953

English for Careers: Business, Professional, and Technical by Leila R. Smith, 8th Edition, Prentice Hall (geared primarily to business) ISBN 013093447X

BOOKS ABOUT USABILITY THAT APPLY TO WEB AND PRESENTATION DESIGN

In addition to learning new kinds of writing skills, those of us in multimedia writing must also become familiar with some basic design principles. Here are some writer-friendly books to help:

The Design of Everyday Things by Donald A. Norman, Currency/Doubleday, reissue edition (February 1990), ISBN 0465067107

Terrific Training Materials: High Impact Graphic Designs (For Workbooks, Handouts, Instructor Guides & Job Aids) by Darlene Frank, HRD Press, ISBN 0874253152

Visual Language: Global Communication for the 21st Century by Robert E. Horn, MacroVU, Inc., ISBN 189263709X

Don't Make Me Think: A Common Sense Approach to Web Usability by Steve Krug and Roger Black, Que, ISBN 0789723107

Designing Web Usability: The Practice of Simplicity by Jakob Nielsen, New Riders Publishing, ISBN 156205810X

Homepage Usability: 50 Websites Deconstructed by Jakob Nielsen, Marie Tahir, New Riders Publishing, ISBN 073571102X

Multimedia and Hypertext: The Internet and Beyond by Jakob Nielsen, Academic Press, reprint edition (February 1995), ISBN 0125184085

Redesigning Print for the Web: Successful Strategies and Professional Techniques for Re-thinking Information Design by Mario R. Garcia, Hayden Books, ASIN 1568303432

JOURNALS AND PERIODICALS

These address multimedia in the context of education, communications, usability, and design:

Journal of Educational Multimedia and Hypermedia (JEMH), ISSN 10558896, www.aace.org/pubs/jemh/default.htm

Journal of Technology and Teacher Education (JTATE), ISSN 10597069, www.aace.org/pubs/jtate/default.htm

Theoretical Foundations of Multimedia, www.uky.edu/~rst/mmbook/ (Also now a book and CD published in 1998 by W. H. Freeman & Co., ISBN 0716783215

JOURNAL ARTICLE

Baker, E. A. The nature of literacy in a technology-rich, fourth-grade classroom. *Reading Research and Instruction*, Volume 40, Number 3 (Spring 2001) page 159. This observation study of a fourth-grade class of 26 students found that technology has changed the nature of literacy. Among its findings: literacy activities are more cooperative and "public"; students used sources and created compositions using special effects unlike those in "traditional" curricula; reading and writing are now more transitory; and publishing is much easier, but may come at the expense of deeper, more thoughtful work.

Glossary

Acronym A word formed from initials, such as KIA for Killed In Action (see chapter 5).

Address The uniform resource locator (URL) for a Website, such as www.specialspecies.com (see chapter 4).

Adjectives Describe nouns and pronouns, such as *beautiful, these, many* (see chapter 5).

Adverbs Mainly describe verbs and adverbs, such as *always, happily, too* (see chapter 5).

ARPANET The original Internet, founded in conjunction with the U.S. military and university research departments in the late 1960s (see chapter 1).

Articles The three adjectives used to describe "which one," such as *a, an, the* (see chapter 5).

Conjunctions Join words or groups of words, such as *and, so, until* (see chapter 5).

Copy Words, text, or other written content (see chapter 1).

Copyright The legal protection afforded an intellectual property, such as original text and images (see chapter 4).

Costuming Visually presenting text in the most effective way (see chapter 7).

Dash Two hyphens (or the equivalent); used to separate words or phrases (see chapter 5).

Domain name The part of the Web address that usually reflects the title of a Website (see chapter 4).

Emphasis Using special effects to draw attention to sentences, phrases, and/or words (see chapter 7).

Fact sheet A written document containing all the information that must be included in a presentation's script (see chapter 10).

Fair use Legal provisions that allow you to use another's material for personal, educational, and noncommercial reasons (see chapter 4).

Fragment An incomplete sentence lacking a subject or verb (see chapter 5).

Goals What you hope to impart to your viewers and the subject matter you will use to achieve that objective (see chapter 2).

Graphical user interface (GUI; pronounced gooey) GUIs allow us to see visuals on the Internet rather than just text (see chapter 1).

Home page The first page of a Website (see chapter 4).

Hypertext Clickable links from one section to another, generally delineated with an underline and color different from the rest of the text (see chapter 1).

Hypertext markup language (HTML) The primary coding language used by anyone writing a Website for the Internet. XML is a newer HTML-like language (see chapter 1).

Hyphen Half a dash; used in many compound words and numbers (see chapter 5).

Image The concept, character, or personification you wish to project through your presentation (see chapter 6).

Images Photographs or graphics (see chapter 1).

Interactivity Communication among people using the tools of the Internet (see chapter 9).

Internet A global network of computers that allows confidential and nonclassified files of information to be transmitted and shared worldwide (see chapter 9).

Inverted pyramid style A journalism convention for organizing content from the most important first to the least important information last (see chapter 8).

Jargon Terminology particular to a certain profession (see chapter 5).

Multimedia Any presentation combining copy, images, sound, motion, and usually hypertext. Output is to a computer screen rather than to paper (see chapter 1).

Multimedia writing Writing for a computer screen (see chapter 3).

Negative space Also called white space, it is an area that is intentionally devoid of content or images (see chapter 8).

Nouns Name persons, places, and things, such as *man*, *Paris*, *happiness* (see chapter 5).

Objectives Based on the knowledge you want your viewers to gain, the feelings and attitudes you want them to develop, and the skills you want them to acquire (see chapter 2).

PDF A file that can be downloaded to be read offline or saved as a file. Created by Adobe Acrobat software, which offers a free PDF Reader that you can download (see chapter 2 and Appendix A for more information on the software program).

Plagiarism The illegal act of stealing the words and/or images conceived by another human being and claiming them as one's own (see chapter 4).

Prepositions Relate position to a noun or pronoun, such as *inside, near, around* (see chapter 5).

Pronouns Substitute for nouns, such as *it, she, they* (see chapter 5).

Resource slide The final presentation slide that lists all the sources or sites from which information or copyrighted images were taken (see chapter 10).

Sans serif font A typeface without "tails" (*sans* is a French word meaning without) (see chapter 7).

Script All the words in your presentation (see chapter 10).

Scrolling Using a navigation device to roll up or down a long Web page (see chapter 9).

Serif font A typeface with a finishing stroke, or a little "tail" leading to the next letter (see chapter 7).

Slang Words, phrases, or terms that reflect a particular culture or group (see chapter 5).

Special effects Methods of making words stand out (see chapter 7).

Tone The mood and overall character of the presentation (see chapter 6).

Too gray A presentation that looks too text-heavy (see chapter 7).

Traditional writing Writing for paper (see chapter 3).

Usability The ease with which a Website is navigated and understood; also called functionality (see chapter 9).

Verbs Action words, such as *run, jump, enjoy* (see chapter 5).

Web page Any single page of a Website (see chapter 4).

Website The entire collection of Web pages and the home page (see chapter 4).

World Wide Web One aspect of the Internet that contains primarily nonclassified governmental, commercial, educational, and organizational electronic files displayed within constructs called Websites (see chapter 9).

Index